Includes
50
Team
Meetings!

THE MEN'S MINISTRY PLAYBOOK

A Proven Strategy to Impact Men

JIM RAMOS

Copyright © 2023 by Jim Ramos

All rights reserved, including the right to reproduce this book or portions thereof in any form whatsoever. For information, you can contact us at **info@meninthearena.org**.

Men in the Arena can bring speakers to your organization to teach the principles covered in this book. For more information, or to book an event, visit us online at **meninthearena.org**.

Cover Design by Caitlin Gipson
Interior Design by Upriver Writing LLC
Manufactured in the United States of America
ISBN: 978-1-961571-07-5

All chapter entries are listed in order according to where they appear in Scripture. Unless noted the entries are from the New American Standard Version (NASB 1995).

THE MEN'S MINISTRY PLAYBOOK

A Proven Strategy to Impact Men

Jim Ramos

with Ken Watson

Men's ministry leader, this book is dedicated to you.
Holding this book means you are a member of the Men in the Arena army, locking shields with thousands of men from around the world who have decided to get out of the anonymous bleachers and into the arena. We applaud you for your courage to build biblical masculinity in the face of a culture that calls it toxic. You stand against the odds. You battle for the hearts of men with less than half a percent of the church budget dedicated to your mission.
You are swimming upriver. You are going against the flow, because you know what many do not: that in Scripture,
God almost always starts with men.
Men are God's starting place.
Thank you for your faithful service.
You are one of my heroes!

> **WHEN A MAN GETS IT—EVERYONE WINS!**

Men in the Arena Tagline

MORE RESOURCES BY JIM RAMOS

FOR YOUR LIBRARY - AVAILABLE ON AMAZON

Strong Men Dangerous Times: Five Essentials Every Man Must Possess to Change His World (Also on Audible)
Guts and Manhood: Four Irrefutable Attributes of Courage (Also on Audible)
The Field Guide: A Bathroom Book for Men (A Daily Devotional)

DOWNLOADABLE BOOKS - AVAILABLE AT MENINTHEARENA.ORG

Tell Them: What Great Fathers Tell Their Sons and Daughters
Help! I'm Starting a Men's Group
ManLaws: 101 Ways to Get Your Man Card Revoked (and Rules to Live By)

FOR YOUR MEN'S GROUP - AVAILABLE ON AMAZON

Strong Men Series Book I: The Trailhead: Protecting Integrity
Strong Men Series Book II: The Climb: Fighting Apathy
Strong Men Series Book III: The Summit: Pursuing God Passionately
Strong Men Series Book IV: The Descent: Leading Courageously
Strong Men Series Book V: The Trail's End: Finishing Strong
Men's Ministry Playbook: A Proven Strategy to Impact Men

If you are in the military, law enforcement, a first responder, a missionary, or a man in an underdeveloped nation please visit meninthearena.org/free for free digital access to all small group resources.

TABLE OF CONTENTS

OF FISH AND MEN	13
WHEN YOU ASSUME...	16

SECTION I: YOUR MEN'S MINISTRY — 17-48

A Proven Strategy: Make it Yours	18
Your Pastor: Role and Responsibility	21
Your Core: The Leadership Team	23
Your Strategy: A Target to Shoot At	25
Your Chosen: Strategic Selection	27
Your Process: Time-Tested Launch Steps	30
Your Rules: Guidelines for Success	33
Your Gathering: Team Meeting Agenda	36
Your Effectiveness: Coaching Tips	38
Your Closer: Great "And One" Questions	47

SECTION II: YOUR MEETINGS — 49-195

Meetings 1-9: Nine Traits of Manhood	52
Meetings 10-11: PMS (Passive Male Syndrome)	70
Meetings 12-17: Guardrails	78
Meetings 18-19: Man Up	94
Meetings 20-22: Lead from the Back	98
Meetings 23-26: Upswept Corners	108
Meetings 27-30: Protect the Ball	120
Meetings 31-33: Iron Men	128
Meetings 34-36: Wild Side	138
Meetings 37-42: In Men, We Trust	150
Meetings 43-46: Tip of the Spear	168
Meetings 47-50: Wisdom Hunters	182

DIVIDE AND CONQUER: DO IT AGAIN	196

Acknowledgments

> **AS MEN GO, SO GOES THE CULTURE.**
>
> Jeff Voth

THE MEN'S MINISTRY PLAYBOOK

OF FISH AND MEN

"Please Lord, one more fish, and I will leave," I guiltily prayed on Father's Day evening of 2023. The wind that weekend had been torrential and for whatever reason (it is fishing not catching) my sons and I failed to catch one fish that represented the species respectably. The Lower Deschutes is famously known for its Redside Rainbow Trout— their broad crimson sides, football-like girth, and ferocious fighting ability due to the fast-running waters of the premier white water rafting place in the Pacific Northwest.

It was dusk and my sons had left earlier that afternoon to be with their loved ones. Staying at our North Central Oregon cabin to write this book, I decided to drive down to the river for the evening caddis hatch in hopes of at least getting good trout to rise to my fly.

With the lowest of expectations, I cast the Blue Olive Dunn imitation that decorated my fly rod. At least I would get to spend time with God, admire the herd of bighorn sheep grazing in the volcanic rock above me, and hopefully catch an epic sunset on the Deschutes River.

A fish would be a welcome bonus.

With two hours left until sunset, the fish began to rise where they were absent the day before when fishing with the boys. Not one fish netted.
Fish on!

What happened next was nothing short of a gift from God. What my sons and I failed to do in three days, I exceeded in less than an hour, netting six gorgeous Redsides, one being the largest to date. Every fish that rose to my fly was hooked was landed, no small miracle as any dry fly fisherman will tell you.

At that moment, knee-deep in the shadows of Deschutes River, I realized what Peter must have felt after an unsuccessful night of fishing only to have the Carpenter call up a netful from the boat ramp!

I began to feel guilty for my son Darby who fished by my side for hours on end with little to show it but a few undersized trout.

To watch a three-pound trout explode out of the water to smash a dry fly is nothing short of addicting. Everything was clicking. I was fully alive. Immersed in the moment. Captured by a fly fisherman's dream. With an hour left of fishing light remaining, I decided to sear the moment in my mind instead of pursuing the fish lust that was tempting me.

"Please Lord, one more and I will leave."
Fish on!

I will never forget two things about that lonely night on Father's Day. How guilty I felt about telling my sons about the experience since they put in the time but I reaped the reward. And how my bride reminded me that I received the greatest Father's Day gift from the greatest Father of all on that evening.

I'm writing this from a picnic bench reflecting on that June evening not far from where I experienced that unforgettable moment. The wind is ripping through the junipers and echoing off the canyon walls. Water answers back by crashing over the boulders to my west.

Out here I have concluded that masculinity, biblical masculinity, and fishing are similar. We hit the water with one goal in mind—to be successful at our craft—but hope the information we've gathered, the right timing, and the presentation is enough to get it done. We read the waters of life and throw everything in our arsenal at it hoping something sticks.

But for many, it is just a guess. Others grow up with examples of masculinity in their lives but at some point, must cast themselves into the currents of life. Still for those with no human example of faith in Someone bigger than themselves, it is an act of futility.

For those who follow the Fisher of men, manhood is a pursuit just as pursuing Christ is one's greatest adventure.

Jesus encouraged his followers to, "Seek first His kingdom and His righteousness and all these things will be added to you as well" (Matthew 6:33). The seeking is what makes faith in Jesus so exhilarating. Like fishing, the pursuit never ends.

We seek Him and we pursue Him with everything in our arsenal (Jeremiah 29:11-13[JP1]) expectant for those moments when we experience Him deeply, yet must choose to trust Him nonetheless, no matter what obstacles drift our way.

Whether you are a pastor, a men's ministry leader looking for another way to disciple men, or just a dude who is committed to personal growth, thank you! Thank you for choosing to make your world better because you are dedicated to it.

When a man gets it—everyone wins.

THE MEN'S MINISTRY PLAYBOOK
WHEN YOU ASSUME...

You've probably heard the saying, "When you assume you make an..." but I am going to assume anyway. There are three assumptions I'm making about who is reading this book.

Assumption #1: You are a man. I made a vow to the Lord that for the rest of my life, everything I write and speak will target men, even when women are in the audience. When writing, I deal with man-specific issues. I get so bored of the authors who write about generic topics and call them men's ministry. Topics like Bible study, prayer, fellowship, and holiness are great topics but are not man-specific enough, so we weave them throughout our writing, but you will not see these topics as the sole focus of our studies. Our topics of study deal with things specific to men.

Assumption # 2: You want to grow spiritually. This book is written for men who are hungry or curious about God. We are all on a spiritual journey and some are further along than others. No matter where you are on your journey, that is great! You are welcome here. This material is written specifically for men who want to grow in the Christian faith. If you are antagonistic about Jesus or could care less about growing spiritually, then this is probably not the book for you.

Assumption #3: You are a pastor, church leader, team (small group) leader, or team member. Since this book contains fifty weeks of curriculum, plus the recipe to start a men's ministry in your church, there is no other reason for a guy to read this unless he is considering involvement in our ministry. I've written many great books for men to read or listen to for pleasure and personal growth that you can check out on our website at meninthearena.org. This book, however, is utilitarian. It was written to get you or your men's ministry rolling! So, if you fit into these three assumptions, welcome to the *Men's Ministry Playbook*!

SECTION I: YOUR MEN'S MINISTRY

THE MEN'S MINISTRY PLAYBOOK

A PROVEN STRATEGY: MAKE IT YOURS

Derrick and Keelie have been supporting our ministry in a big way since leaving the vocational ministry to enter the workforce. Every year they give a large sum of money, based on the income from the business they own. One day I was having a meal with Derrick and thanked him for their more than generous offerings. "Oh, that is not my idea!" Derrick immediately announced. "We give because my wife saw how it single-handedly transformed our church."

Derrick and Keelie ministered in a small rural church for many years until one day they were confronted by the eldership that they needed to focus more of their efforts on men. Searching for a ministry model that fit their vision for men, he reached out to our organization and the eldership went all in. When I say "all in" I mean it. The elders of this small church partnered up and launched our ministry with their sweat equity, strategically staggering three teams (small groups) and committing three years to build our system.

This is not an easy task. There is no easy way to transform anything, let alone the men of a church!

On any given Sunday there are 13 million more adult women in America's churches than men. Of those men, Patrick Morley in *The Christian Man* states that only 1 in 12 men is part of a community group. Almost 25 percent of married, churchgoing women will worship without their husbands. Midweek activities often draw 70 to 80 percent female participants, while the men opt out. Most church employees are women, except for the pastoral team, who are overwhelmingly male.

Churches overseas report gender gaps of up to nine women for every adult man in attendance. The typical Christian college in the U.S. enrolls almost two women for every man. And fewer than 10 percent of U.S. churches can establish or maintain a vibrant men's ministry.

Back to the story.

Three years later, without any other strategic changes, their church grew in attendance to two services, increased giving, and men in volunteer ministry roles. Experts estimate that the average church attendance in America is about 39% male compared to 51% of regular church attendees being women, which explains the pastel foyers, flowers on the stage, bright lighting, and overly heated sanctuary.

Two remarkable things happened in their church that they were not expecting. With the strategic shift of focus, men dominated church attendance at well over 50%. The second made me laugh. The women began complaining about the men's ministry being so impactful that they rallied, and the women's ministry exploded!

This proves what I've been saying for years, "When a man gets it—everyone wins!"

Your church does not need another men's breakfast or service project. It needs a strategic, transformative, movement so impactful that the women will want a piece of it!

A study from Hartford Seminary found that the presence of involved men was statistically correlated with church growth, health, and harmony. Meanwhile, a lack of male participation is strongly associated with congregational decline (C. Kirk Hadaway, FACTS on Growthy: A New Look at the Dynamics of Growth and Decline in American Congregations Based on Faith Communities Today. 2005 national survey of Congregations. Hartford Institute for Religion).

In the *Men's Ministry Playbook*, we will not guarantee transformation like Derrick and Keelie saw in their church. And I will never tell you it is easy. Change never is. I'm a horrible salesman. But what I will tell you is that this book provides a strategy to reach and disciple men as well as fifty team meetings, which is about two church years (September to June) of ministry—one year if you choose to burn them up with no summer break, which is a bad idea.

Most churches are failing to engage and transform most men. Though many churches are led by men and have a cadre of dedicated mature men, most men in those churches remain apathetic spectators rather than living like the Bible describes and commands. Don't be content with a small minority of active disciples among the men of your church!

The Bible studies in this book have been used to transform large numbers of men into passionate Christ-followers. Men who previously resisted serving in their churches are now becoming servant-leaders in the ministries of their churches. Men who previously preferred to let their wives act as family spiritual leaders are making disciples within their own families. Men who were in bondage to anger, porn, and materialism are living in victorious integrity.

The 50 Bible studies in this book are designed for use in squads of 6-15 men meeting weekly under the leadership of two captains. Every meeting gives explicit attention to the needs and growth of each man and is based on scriptures that have set men on fire for God. The topics and language are for men. Men who have experienced this program (and their wives) are passionate about the difference it has made in their lives and their churches.

Here is one guarantee that you can take to the bank. If the plan you implement among your men's community is ours and not yours, you are setting yourself up for failure. You need to own it. Make it yours. By yours, I mean your pastor, elders, and your men's ministry team (more on this later).

You are not in this alone. I encourage you to carefully read through the coaching tips section, especially join our Men in the Arena Leadership message thread, Equipping Blast, and monthly Virtual Training call with men's leaders like you from around the world.

Make it yours.

THE MEN'S MINISTRY PLAYBOOK

YOUR PASTOR: ROLE AND RESPONSIBILITY

We've seen some Lead Pastors who are so passionate about the value of discipling men that they form their own Men's Small Groups under their leadership. Some of those pastors are using the Bible studies of this book with great effect! But be aware that to lead one such group effectively will require an investment of several hours a week for a typical church ministry year from September to mid-June—thirty weeks, give or take.

And for many churches, you need not one such group, but multiple groups meeting at different times and places that fit into the lives of men. This is where your leadership team plays a critical role. Also, many pastors have seen groups take on an even more transforming impact when they are led by two non-ministry professionals.

In the previous story, Derrick never led or joined a men's team but the men's ministry thrived nonetheless. Why? Because he implemented simple, yet catalytic things that led to his success. Here are some critical areas where you can come alongside the men of your church.

Attitude.
Change it. Bold men in the church can be intimidating to an insecure pastor but it does not need to be that way. The strong men of your congregation are assets, not liabilities. Partner with them in spirit. Think of the impact of one changed man on his household. Read the book of Acts. Look at the numbers. When you get the man, you almost always get the entire family. Not so with the women. When a man gets it—everyone wins.

Adjust.
Your focus must change from everyone to men. That's right. When you speak, craft your message to the men and the women will follow. If you speak to and target the women, the men will leave. The way you dress needs to fit the average man in your church. No long flowing robes! Get out of the Middle Ages! Change your language to fit the average man.

I did a wedding recently and was complimented by the father of the groom that I had a way of taking complex Bible words and making them easy to explain. It wasn't hard. I also speak to men, even when women are present. Much of what pastors do is teach the Bible. Use the power of story and object lessons to connect with the visual learners in the audience, the men.

Alter.

This will take time, but when the leader changes his attitude and adjusts his focus, the next logical step is to alter the physical appearance of the church. Put magazine racks above the urinals. Decorate them with masculine colors and decorations. Dim the lights in your sanctuary. Reduce the temperature to 68 degrees. Use earth tones instead of pastels. Reject all anti-biblical and feminine lyrics from worship. You get the point.

Announce and Attend.

Prioritize men's events in the bulletin and weave them into your sermon. Be a cheerleader for the men of your church. Then attend the events. All of them. Larger churches should mandate full participation at all men's events for male staff. While I'm at it, you can be absent from your church building one Sunday a year to attend the annual (always awesome and well-funded) men's retreat.

Act.

Besides attending men's ministry events (Hey, I'm permitting you to skip women's ministry events!), verbally bless the men's ministry. Receiving a blessing from the pastor gives your men the boost they need to keep pressing on. Imitate The Father, Moses, Jesus, and Paul by publicly commissioning any men who start a men's group. Lastly, if you are like most churches, your men receive less than ½% of the annual budget for men's ministry. Make it your mission to increase that number to 2%.

THE MEN'S MINISTRY PLAYBOOK

YOUR CORE: THE LEADERSHIP TEAM

To have a transforming men's ministry, a leadership team is essential. Giving all the Men's Ministry Leadership to one man is a recipe for an unsuccessful leader and for an unsuccessful ministry. Men achieve best when they are part of a team that shares the ministries and goals!

We recommend at least a 3-man leadership team. Each member of the team can have a focused responsibility but should consult with the rest of the team in his leadership area. Any church larger than 100 in average weekly attendance can accomplish this with little effort. Before we dive into our suggested leadership team titles and responsibilities, I want to share some common assumptions and expectations of your core team.

They need to be committed followers of Jesus and committed assets in your church. They should be men. Duh. They should be expected to attend most of the men's events, which should be no more than 4-6 a year including the men's retreat.

Leading or co-leading a men's team (small group) is not an option. They must all lead or co-lead a men's small group. Here are the men who make your leadership team.

The Leader.
The buck must stop with someone, and that someone is the leader. The Men's Ministry Leader works with the pastor, elders, and Men's Leadership Team to set the vision, and budget, and coordinate calendared events with the church calendar. He will run the Leadership Team meetings and stay close to the men on his leadership team. He will work with the Events Guy to plan the annual men's retreat weekend.

The Admin Guy.
By necessity, The Admin Guy is the second in charge. Where the leader's role is on the macro or big picture scale, The Admin Guy leads on a micro level. He manages the budget, receipts for events, church bulletin announcements, speaker honorariums, branding, and marketing.

I cannot survive without this person and in full-time ministry since 1990 have always found a person to fit this role, whether paid or volunteer. This role has changed my life. I married this person!

The Events Guy.

His role is to work with the Leader to plan 4-6 events a year. We suggest erring on the side of lesser to establish long-term credibility. The men's retreat weekend is one of those events. You have a lot of freedom when planning these events. In my experiences, I have seen men's breakfasts, service days, shooting, rafting, golf, lake days, minigolf, go-carts, bonfires, a rite of passage, and snowmobiling. Snowboarding/skiing, Frisby golf, fishing, the sky is the limit.

Blend fun with discipleship and service. Your goal should be to build relationships among the men and a sense of connectedness and community.

Teams Guy.

Every group needs a Navy SEAL. This is the small group coordinator. The functional ministry core of your men's ministry is not events. ***Churches fail when they build a men's ministry around events. This is a massive mistake.***

Instead, build your ministry around a core team of leaders who are committed, like in Derrick's story, to pay the price of sweat equity for their men and that sweat is poured out through small groups. The Teams Guy recruits team leaders and uses our seven-step launch system to train them, as well as establishing communication threads like texting, Telegram, or Messenger so leaders can stay always connected.

The Utility Player(s).

The sky is the limit to the number of men on your leadership team if each man fills a role. No titles. No talkers. Only doers. I think Mel Gibson's character, William Wallace, said it best, "People don't follow titles. They follow courage." I recently had to fire four volunteers for talking about leading but not following through with their leadership commitments. Yes, I fired volunteers! Utility players lead or co-lead a group plus do things like take care of refreshments, cook, or plan a specific event. You get the picture.

There you go! Now you have exactly what you need to strategically launch a men's ministry in your church community.

THE MEN'S MINISTRY PLAYBOOK

YOUR CHOSEN: STRATEGIC SELECTION

As I write this, our organization, Men in the Arena, has reached men in every state in America, 168 nations, and in January 2022 became the number one podcast for Christian Men on Spotify. As our ministry continues explosive growth to the glory of God, I am blown away that the ministry launched with fifteen men in a coffee shop in the small agricultural community of McMinnville, Oregon; one of the least churched states per capita in America (New Hampshire residents claim the #1 position, but they are wrong!).

Those fifteen men were selected from my church using the 5 C's approach. Before I get into what those are I want to address an unwritten rule for selection. As an organization, we are driven by a vision, mission, Critical Success Factors, and values. Our values act as guardrails or boundaries limiting our audience. They keep us in our lane so to speak. One of those is Strategic Partnerships meaning, "We believe in forming strategic partnerships with diverse, Christ-centered people, and organizations around the world, that will ultimately put Jesus on display."

Why am I sharing this? When at all possible, you should select your men from a diverse group demographically, vocationally, ethnically, chronologically, and even politically as we will see a bit later. I love the church and the various people that God brings together!

Here are the 5 C'S I looked for in recruiting those original fifteen men.

Christ.
Because I follow Jesus and write to Christian men, my selection process began with men who were in my local church. That being said, Jesus selected Judas who was not on Team Jesus. In my original group, we selected a man who was not committed to Jesus, but that soon changed, and his wife became one of the biggest evangelists for our organization. Your group should have one or two men who are "projects" that you see with great potential if Jesus got ahold of them.

Character.

I want to spend time shaping men of high moral character and not some dirtbag who only cares about getting ahead by any means necessary. Does that sound exclusive? You bet it does. We all struggle and are all sinners but if a man is hungry to change, he is a prime recruit. I am not interested in recruiting men who could care less about becoming a man of high moral character. A man does not have to know Jesus to be a man of character. Conversely, a man may claim to follow Jesus but lack integrity in many ways.

Competency.

I recruited men who were competent in their careers, who understood what it meant to follow Jesus (though not always doing it), and who were intellectually similar to the men in the group which leads to the next C.

Chemistry.

This is where it gets a little tricky biblically. Let me explain. Of the Twelve, Jesus chose Simon the Zealot, a militant Jew committed to restoring the nation of Israel through violence and overthrowing the Roman government, and Matthew, a Jew who rejected the Mosaic law to work for the Romans extorting taxes from fellow Jews. They couldn't have been more politically polarized. Somehow Jesus pulled it off, and we never hear of conflict between those men. The challenge is to recruit a diverse group of men who have the potential for great chemistry—men who like each other and connect regardless of their differences.

Commitment.

Men must commit upfront to attend 75% or more team meetings. Anything less is unacceptable and grounds for removal. The temptation is when you find a top-shelf man who is unwilling to commit because of his busy schedule. Reject that man. He is not a good fit for your group. Men must know this upfront. I would rather have a group of C+ men with Grade A hearts than A+ quality men with C+ commitment all day long.

THE MEN'S MINISTRY PLAYBOOK

YOUR STRATEGY: A TARGET TO SHOOT AT

When it comes to your annual calendar, less is more. Do not make the mistake that so many inexperienced, yet zealous men's leaders make and pack your calendar with events and no strategic ways to move men forward in their spiritual journey. I want to restate something I said earlier. The most important programming element of your men's ministry is not your men's retreat weekend, breakfast, or some other monthly or quarterly event. It is the team (a.k.a. small group). It is best to describe the strategy using a hybrid of Rick Warren's material from Purpose Driven Church where he broke the Great Commission (Matthew 28:16-20) and the Greatest Commandment (Matthew 22:35-37) into five purposes of the church: ministry, fellowship, discipleship, worship, and evangelism.

Bull's Eye. Imagine a target. The bull's eye, of course, is the Christ—Jesus. He is the central figure of everything we do! We even added an "X" or cross to make the spot!

Ministry Purpose.
Working from the bull's eye outward the next concentric circle is your Core (aka Leadership Team). The biblical purpose for your leadership core is ministry. In other words, the primary purpose of this group is service. Although Christian fellowship is a wonderful byproduct of this group, the purpose is a ministry more than fellowship, which is why every man must play a role. Because your Leadership Team members are also team leaders, there is no need to meet unless necessary. This is a working task force more than an advisory committee. I cannot stress this enough. The only time our team officially meets is in the months leading up to the annual Men's Retreat Weekend since there are so many moving parts.

As we move outward through our circles it is important to note that no purpose stands alone when talking about ministry. Because we are living, breathing, souls in pursuit of our Savior every activity planned has to oscillate between two or more purposes. For example, the purpose of small group teams is fellowship, but discipleship is an equally important purpose of these groups and should never be neglected.

Fellowship Purpose.
The third ring from the center is the purpose of fellowship for the committed. What are they committed to? All team members commit to meeting no less than 75% of all meetings and buy-in to the group by purchasing any small group resources needed such as the Men's Ministry Playbook in your hand. This is crucial. Men need to buy in to increase commitment to the team. If any man cannot afford the book price, make them earn it through sweat equity. Do not let a man in without him first paying the price.

Bible study is the tool used to minister to men during the team meeting—discipleship—but fellowship is a must for your team. Your team meetings are split between the two purposes of fellowship and discipleship. Without fellowship, your men lack a spiritual purpose for spiritual growth. As the core ministry focus of your men's strategy, small groups meet weekly during the church year (September to June).

Discipleship Purpose.
The fourth circle from the center is discipleship. Discipleship is a weekly commitment that is half of your team meeting's focus as mentioned above. The discipleship purpose splits its time between team meetings and weekly church service. We live in a time when the local church is under scrutiny. Many believers have left the local church, which I believe is detrimental in the long run. I have yet to meet a Christian man who is not plugged into a local church community who is thriving spiritually. Although many of your men may not be committed to the local church, your goal should be for every man to eventually plug in for reasons I will not go into here.

Worship Purpose.
The fifth ring from the center is worship. The primary mode of worship is provided by the local church, although Shanna may disagree. She has worship playing 24/7 in our home and car. She connects with God through worship whereas I tend to connect with God through prayer and Bible study. By worship I am talking about connecting with God through music with the ultimate goal to worship God with our lives which is seen through the Greek word *proskuneo*, which means, to pay homage or to kiss, like kissing the hand of a superior. It is commonly associated with bowing down or lying prostrate on the ground with the idea of kissing the ground before someone. Some scholars believe the word is derived from the idea of a dog licking its master's hand. The idea is to show profound reverence and submission to someone (Tyndale).

A man who worships God (*proskuneo*) cannot help but cry out to God through corporate prayer and worship through music. Again, the local church is the goal.

Evangelism Purpose.
So far, we've discussed five rings of your men's ministry strategy, the biblical purposes of each, and the commitment required—Christ, Core (ministry), Committed (fellowship/discipleship), and Church (discipleship/worship). The sixth and final circle of your ministry to men is **evangelism** or outreach. This is where your quarterly event and men's retreat weekend play a role. They are designed to pull men into the ministry from those filling anonymous chairs in church and the men in the community who are committed to not attending church.

Let me explain. One of my dirty pleasures in life is Burger King's famous Whoppers (no onions please, and yes please, on the fries and Diet Coke!). They are the standard by which I measure all burgers. Imagine that one day you are in Burger King minding. Your own business, and I walked in shouting, "I am a Whopper. I am a Whopper!"

What would you do? You would medicate me, place me in a straitjacket, and haul me away! Attending church and thinking you are a devoted follower of Jesus isn't much different than thinking I am a BK Whopper!

What's your point, Jim? My point is that our churches are packed with anonymous men who are committed to not committing their time, talents, or resources to the work of God's Kingdom. For whatever reason, they are content with sporadic church attendance, minimal commitment, and anonymity. They show up late but make up for it by leaving early!

They need to be strategically and methodically targeted by your men's ministry.

THE MEN'S MINISTRY PLAYBOOK

YOUR PROCESS: TIME-TESTED LAUNCH STEPS

Over the last decade, this process has substantially evolved to fit those launching local teams as well as post-pandemic virtual teams. The process was inspired by Robert E. Coleman's classic work, *The Master Plan of Evangelism*, "It is rather startling to observe in the Gospels that these early disciples did not do much more than watch Jesus work for a year or two. He did not ask anyone to do or be anything he had first not demonstrated in his own life. It is well enough to tell people what we mean, but it is infinitely better to show them how to do it. People are looking for a demonstration, not an explanation."

The leadership development process has evolved the several launch steps in this book. If you have questions or issues, please email us anytime at info@meninthearena.org and one of our coaches will reach out to you ASAP.

Launch Step One: Recruit a Co-Leader.
This will be a theme throughout the course of this book. Jesus paired up The Disciples. You have a co-leader. And you will pair up the men on your team. Although it is not mandatory that you do this to launch a team, we highly recommend that you have another man to lock shields with through this process. There will be times when you can't make it to the team meeting, and it's good to know that someone has your back. Besides recruiting team members, leaders often confess that finding their co-captain was the most challenging step in launching a new team. If you already have your co-captain, great job!

When recruiting a potential team captain to use our material, please send him to our website (meninthearena.org). Second, encourage him to get support from our many online resources, including our monthly virtual training for all leaders and our leadership messenger thread where your questions and prayer requests will be answered immediately. Once you have your co-captain, move to Launch Step Two.

Launch Step Two: Build Your Hit Lists.
Did you know that in Luke 6:12-16 we discover that Jesus recruited The Twelve Disciples from a larger group of disciples? Check it out:

*"One of those days Jesus went out to a mountainside to pray and spent the night praying to God. When morning came, **he called his disciples to him and chose twelve of them**, whom he also designated apostles: Simon (whom he named Peter), his brother Andrew, James, John, Philip, Bartholomew, Matthew, Thomas, James, son of Alphaeus, Simon who was called the Zealot, Judas son of James, and Judas Iscariot, who became a traitor."*

You and your co-captain will each create a Hit List (two total) of no less than 15 potential recruits on each list. Commit your Hit List to prayer, asking God to direct you through the process.

Once both lists have been compiled, pray over them and decide who will receive a formal "call" (Launch Step Three) to be on your team. Some team captains invite all the men from their Hit Lists while others are more selective. This is a personal preference. Some captains struggle to recruit enough men for their team. Others must cut their Hit List down. Team size should range from a minimum of **eight to twenty members** max. With attrition and weekly absenteeism, you will probably end up with about a dozen men.

If possible, create an intergenerational team of men ranging throughout multiple decades of life. Once the Hit List is created move on to Launch Step Three.

Launch Step Three: The Call.
This is important! You and your co-captain set the meeting day, time, and date, ***then*** call the men. Don't ask the men what they prefer. Decide on inviting men to join your team.

You have two options for your team. First, the team you're building can either be a closed group where men are not allowed to join after a certain time frame, say three weeks. This is my preferred option. The second is to recruit your team but leave it open-ended if men want to invite a buddy or if a man moves into your area or church and is looking for a men's group. Either way is fine. You make the call.

Some men won't be able to join your team simply because of your meeting times. That's normal and you must be okay with it. Here is a potential pitch or elevator speech:

"Hey Joe, this is Mike! I want to talk to you about something that has helped me become the best version of a man through Christ. It is an internationally known Christian organization for men called Men in the Arena. I am so excited about this that I'm starting a team of my own with my friend, (co-leader). I want to invite you to join us. We meet every (day of the week) from (0:00) to (0:00) at (location). Will you come to our first meeting and check it out?" Wait for his answer.

One more thing about The Call. The Call is not a text, email, or message. It is a phone call or face-to-face—preferably face to face where you can look your recruit in the eye and ask him like a man.

Launch Step Four: Team List.
How Captains communicate with their teams is partly what separates the good teams from the great ones. Let me restate that. Communication is what separates great team leaders from average ones. The Team List will be used on the Buy-In (Launch Step Six) and must include: Name (and wife's name if married), e-mail (and wife's e-mail), and cell phone number. Pro-tip. I save each man's name in my contacts along with his wife's name until it is memorized.

The sooner the following lists are created and consistently used the more effective your team will be—E-mail, messenger thread, and/or text group. Use the Team List to remind the men about your weekly meetings. This acts as a reminder and gives men a simple way to reply if they can't make it that week.

Launch Step Five: Team and Spouses Gathering.
You're almost there! You only have a few more steps until your team launches! Great job! We can't over-emphasize the importance of the Couple's gathering, especially for married men. Use your Team (formerly Hit) List to communicate the time and date of the Team and Spouses' Gathering. Your best bet is the same time as your team meeting, but at least three weeks in advance so men have time to order their books. Give your potential team members at least three weeks advance notice and communicate with their wives. We have found that the wives are usually the ones who manage the family calendar.

Your goal is 100% attendance of those invited. Team leaders who opt out of Team Spouses Gathering to hurry the process, have proved it to be a mistake. The goal is to get total buy-in from the wives and have all questions answered. If the wife is in, the man is in. Trust us!

We've seen it over and over. Attendance by the wives is critical for the success of the team. Below is a Team Spouses Gathering potluck sample agenda.

*Potluck
*Team Leader and wife introductions
*Team member and wife introductions
*Review Team Launch information (day, time, and place), commitment level (75% attendance), and other pertinent information
*Explain the Buy-In (Launch Step Six)
*Q and A
*Pray over the group
*Gathering Ends

Launch Step Six: Buy-In.
You can almost taste your team launch at his point. We're as excited as you to see lives transformed through your team! All that's left is to order the books. Attrition will most likely claim some (20%) of the men, but we have found that the more the men buy in, the more committed they will be. This needs to take place at least two weeks before your launch day. You can have the church purchase them or buy them yourself and have the men reimburse you. Or send your men directly to meninthearena.org or Amazon to purchase the curriculum themselves.

Launch Step Seven: Team Leader Commissioning.
Did you know that in the New Testament, the Twelve Apostles, the Apostle Paul—and Jesus himself—were commissioned into ministry? We highly recommend it as a model for spiritual leadership. The sooner this is set up with your pastor the better. The Commission Day should happen 1-2 weeks **before** your team officially launches, preferably by your pastor in a church service. If not, reach out to me and I will personally do it even if it is virtual. It is **that** important!

Thank you so much for getting out of the anonymous bleachers and into the Arena! Again, please lock shield with our organization and resources to help you thrive!

THE MEN'S MINISTRY PLAYBOOK

YOUR RULES: GUIDELINES FOR SUCCESS

I am not a great small group leader. I admit it. Especially when it comes to teaching the Bible or resources I've written, I tend to talk too much and listen too little. It is embarrassing when people I have trained are better than I am at teaching the resources I wrote, and it happens all the time! Great small group leaders have a way of responsive listening, extracting comments from the quiet guys, and diverting the dominating guys.

There are however some critical factors involved in a successful small group.

Dynamics.
Here are three simple yet impactful physical dynamics of every successful group. Watch the 80's hit Breakfast Club for the best scene of an effective small group I have ever witnessed.

One, sit at eye level with no man sitting higher than another (unless he is taller of course).

Two, have team members sit equidistant from the center of the group. No rectangles. Not trapezoids. Not ovals. Circles and squares are your friends.

Third, until you are experienced with your men and leading a small group, allow equal opportunities for participation. In other words, physically look each man in the eye and give them a chance to talk allowing them to pass at any time.

Rules.

These following five rules are simple, but break even one of them, you'll watch men leave your group and never return.

Honesty or Silence

Each man has a chance to answer every question. Don't force anyone to talk. Some men are natural talkers and others are quiet. When men speak demand the truth, but all have the right to either speak or pass.

Respect

It takes courage for some men to speak. We all have a starting place. Disrespect a man and you lose him. Even if an answer is wrong in your opinion, don't disrespect or demean him. Respect is the greatest gift you can give to another man. Remember that!

Confidentiality

What happens in the team meeting stays in the team meeting. It's tough enough to share without the fear that what you share may be shared with others. Please don't mention what is shared in this group with anyone else- especially your wife!

Commitment

The groups have been carefully selected. Please honor that by showing up on time, every time, and participating.

Questions

You don't have to get through every question. The questions are simply a springboard for discussion. Use them if they help. Ignore them if they don't.

THE MEN'S MINISTRY PLAYBOOK

YOUR GATHERING: A TEAM MEETING AGENDA

We launched Men in the Arena in 2012 with 15 men, ages 28-74, meeting from 5:30-6:30 a.m. in a local coffee shop. Most guys showed up early for coffee and fellowship. Our team meetings were short, at only an hour, to honor men who were heading off to work or back home to help with breakfast and get the kiddos ready for school. Our motto was and still is, *"Start on time. End on time. Every time."* This is the mantra for all Men in the Arena groups.

Honor the men, many of whom are living in the Stress Bubble of life—married, having children, serving in their community, and generally building a life and career. Every minute is precious to them. Do not take advantage of one of them.

In the early days, we wrote two curriculum books with a total of 90 meetings, respectively titled Playbooks 1 and 2. We eventually pulled them down, and they became the five-book series, the *Strong Men Series Study Guides*, with 50 total meetings that included a rough agenda and twice as much material per meeting. Interestingly, the men who went through both books gave feedback that they preferred the Bible discussion format in *Playbooks 1 and 2* overwhelmingly more than the copious notes in the *Strong Men Study Guide Series*. thus, the *Men's Ministry Playbook*!

Each of the fifty meetings in this book represents one hour, which should give you close to two church- ministry- years- worth of curriculum, or one year if you grind it out through summer. Men can show up early or stay late, but the meetings are exactly an hour.

Meeting Guideline

Below is a sample guideline for each meeting. Adjust it to meet the needs of your men while keeping within the one-hour parameter.

Opening Prayer (5 mins)

Prayer is the official kick-off of your meeting. It starts on time. Every time. This can be done as a group or simply open in prayer.

Personal Story (10 mins)

Take one week for every man in your group to share his personal faith story. This is the glue that will bond your men together. Something special happens when men connect through their stories. Each man will share his story—one man per week—until all men have shared. You may have to adjust your agenda to make this happen, but it is well worth it.

Hero (aka Victory) Stories (5 mins)

We believe God has placed men to be the hero in their stories. God is the famous One and ultimate Hero, but he has asked men to lead the way in being an example to those who love and trust him for leadership. Hero stories are testimonies where God has used the men in your group to impact lives for Jesus.

Bible Study (30 mins)

Work through the study with your men. Prepare your notes beforehand. This is not a platform for you to teach, preach, or exhibit your great Bible knowledge. It is a time to facilitate the study of God's Word as it relates to masculine themes in Scripture.

Huddle Time and Closing Prayer (10 mins)

The Huddle Time is a time to break into the same smaller groups of 3-4 men each week, answer an "And One" question together, and pray for each other before ending the hour on time. Every time.

THE MEN'S MINISTRY PLAYBOOK

YOUR EFFECTIVENESS: COACHING TIPS

Two by Two

Pairing up his leaders was a strategy Jesus employed. He paired up The Twelve. He sent The Seventy out in pairs. You have a co-leader. You should pair up the men on your team as soon as possible. They will share Huddle Time with another pair and will eventually be asked to launch a team of their own together. But how did Jesus pair up his men? What can we learn from Jesus the leader? His pairs were not random. He had two sets of brothers in Peter and Andrew and the Sons of Thunder pair: James and John. Next in the Luke 6:12-16 list of The Twelve were best friends Philip and Bartholomew (a.k.a. Nathaniel). The final three pairings must have been men with great chemistry but that is my best guess. To evangelize the world, then, Jesus picked two sets of brothers, one set of best bros, and three sets of men who connected on some level (Of course Judas did not make it).

Three Strikes of Confidentiality

Confidentiality is a non-negotiable with our teams. If a man breaks confidentiality, we recommend implementing Church discipline based on Matthew 18. In Matthew 18:15-18 Jesus taught us how to deal with those who sin against us: *"If your brother sins, go and show him his fault in private; if he listens to you, you have won your brother. But if he does not listen to you, take one or two more with you, so that by the mouth of two or three witnesses every fact may be confirmed. If he refuses to listen to them, tell it to the church; and if he refuses to listen even to the church, let him be to you as a Gentile and a tax collector. Truly I say to you, whatever you bind on earth shall have been bound in heaven; and whatever you loose on earth shall have been loosed in heaven."*

Get Support

Men's ministry leaders often share that they feel alone and unsupported. It doesn't have to be that way! When you launch a team, reach out to us at info@meninthearena.org and let us connect you with other leaders of men on our monthly Virtual Men's Ministry leader calls and our Messenger thread so you can get the support you need when you need it.

Team Potluck

This is also called the "Couple's Potluck". It is strategically designed to build team unity and buy-in from the wives. The potluck was our most powerful tool to get the wives behind their husband's discipleship though the overwhelming majority was overjoyed by it. We changed the name to "Team Potluck" since we didn't want to exclude any single or widowed men. Summer is a great time for a team gathering of some kind.

Finish Each Year Strong

Make sure to finish this year strong. Do you have an end-of-the-year event? Do your men know when you kick off in the fall? Will you be adding more men to your team? Do you need to contact absent men?

Sharing Stick

Just kidding. We don't use one but what you're about to hear is critical to the success of your group. Recently, several women have asked how they can start a group where the women share like our Men in the Arena teams (husbands are talking), which was shocking because I wrongly assumed women naturally did this. They do not. The curriculum presented here is outstanding because we do not ask the men to sit passively as a video is played while a spiritual leader teaches. And the leaders are not teachers who regurgitate scripted information. Our team leaders are facilitators who are simply asked to read Bible verses, answer their thoughts on said passage, and ask team members to do the same. TheBottom line is this: do not dominate your team meetings unless, of course, you want to ruin them.

25% Rule

The team Leader should talk no more than 25% of the time. You are NOT the designated "teacher" for the group but a leader and facilitator of it. It's your job to research the lesson, ask great questions, and facilitate Bible study and discussion.

Open-Ended Questions

We've worked hard at asking open-ended questions. Stay on task in doing the same. Avoid "Yes" and "No" answers like the plague. Instead of asking, "Do you struggle with X or Y?" ask, "Where do you struggle the most?" Also, men don't need your arrogant monologue, boring pontifications, or theological dissertations. They need to learn how to study and grow in the world on their own.

When Men Move On

When a man physically moves out of the area, leaves the group, or starts a new team— what do you do? It depends on your current team dynamics. The tension between team numbers and group continuity is powerful. I (Jim) have done several things in the past. If you don't want to change the team dynamics, don't. If you've lost a noticeable number of guys for various reasons you may want to consider pulling new guys in or doing a restart. If your men are close, have shared deeply, and building trust, then you may be wise to leave the group as is.

Feel the Pulse

The morale of the men, and each team, is fluid. How are your team guys doing? Where would you grade the morale and commitment of your team A-F? What is the current pulse of your men? Who's been missing? Who seems disengaged? Who's fired up? Are you connecting with your co-captain? Have you asked them what they think about the morale of the team? Maybe you should?

Commitment

Remember to hold your team members to 75% minimum attendance. That is three out of every four weeks in a month. It's easy to slack off and get out of a rhythm. Make sure you are the most regular attender of your group. The men on your team will only be as committed as you are.

Play the Movie

Your goal is not only to lead your men through the Men in the Arena team meetings but for your men to partner up and start teams of their own after you're through the series of books. Remember everything you do, or fail to do, impacts the multiplication of your team. Keep that future launch date in mind as you lead your team. Prepare your lesson well and scribble notes in the margins so your guys see that you've done your homework. Mentally pair your men up as co-team captains. Talk about that time often so the men get used to hearing that you expect it from them.

Get Equipped Every Week

Make sure to sign up for my weekly Equipping Newsletter, where I write a manhood-related email and present our two podcast episodes for the week. Thousands of men subscribe to this because it is an asset in their lives. Get it at meninthearena.org/newsletter.

Fall Meeting Fumble

If you are struggling as the team leader with getting your men to your fall meetings let me ask you. Have you called each of them? Have you met with any of them? Have you had a fall kick-off event including the wives? Have you consistently attended? Have you shown up on time and prepared?

Be Prepared

Come prepared to lead your team meeting and know who will show up ahead of time. If you haven't done so yet, consider launching this year's team, every year, with a Team (aka Couples) Potluck to get everyone on the same page and make sure the wives are informed.

Three "Ls" of Manhood

There are three general stages of life a man passes through. We have embedded those three phases in our system as well. He grows up in a home (0-25) where he spends his younger years as a learner and family member where he sits under the leadership of his parents. Eventually, he falls in love, marries, and starts a family (25-55). It is then that he enters the Arena (a.k.a. Stress Bubble) of life where he becomes the leader of his family; training, guiding, and serving his family. His children eventually move out and start families of their own, transitioning him from leader to patriarch (55+), legacy leaver. In the third phase, he will spend the majority of his life, sometimes up to half of it, as a guide, coach, and advisor. The goal of all Men in the Arena teams is for men to move through these three phases as well—learner, leader, and legacy leaver.

Hero (a.k.a. Victory) Stories

Men from all over the world are experiencing life change as a result of our ministry. We try to post one Hero Story on some platform every week. 'Hero stories' are stories of life change, transformation, or a decisive act to grow. They aren't messages telling us we are great, but rather about how God has used our ministry to help you make a tangible change. We reward anyone who submits their Hero Story with some swag when we celebrate their story publicly. Please share any Hero Stories you hear with us, as well as pictures of your Men in the Arena team. We love to celebrate what God is doing!

Sit Close Together

Remembering how your men are positioned in the room is everything! The men need to be at eye level and as equidistant from the center or an eight-foot-in diameter circle as possible. If your circle, or any man, is further than four feet from the center your discussions will be greatly hindered.

What Happens in Group...

Remember to protect your men. Follow the Las Vegas rule, "What happens in our meetings...stays in our meetings." Asking for forgiveness instead of asking for permission is a juvenile way of thinking. Unless permission is given ahead of time do not share stories from your team meetings, post pics of your team praying over specific men, or anything that may breach the Vegas rule. Maintain the confidentiality, integrity, and trust of your men, and avoid anything that may breach the Vegas rule.

Remember the Big Picture

People ask us all the time who is Men in the Arena and what is our vision and mission. Here are our three-tier vision and missions. Our Vision is to see a growing army of men, who are becoming their best version and changing their world. Our Mission is to inspire, equip, and mobilize men to transform their lives, the people they love, and the communities they impact.

Send a Team Picture

We, at Men in the Arena love to celebrate every victory God gives us. Whenever a new team starts, we get pumped because we know the power of a team of men locking shields together (whether it be one of our real-time to virtual teams). If you are on a Men in the Arena team, please send us your team pic so we can post it on all our media outlets!

Visit Our Website for Training Videos

As you prepare to start a Men in the Arena team (real-time or virtual) make sure you check our website at meninthearena.org. We have some amazing resources for you including videos designed to help you launch your new team, a backlog of podcast episodes, and a myriad of free resources for you,

Summer Fun

Life is full and summer is a good time to exhale for a season and take a break from your weekly team meetings. We're all busy but anything you can do to get the wives and your men together will only help forge a deeper bond with each other. A good summer approach now that your team is not meeting is to connect over the summer with one or two summer events.

Subscribe to the Men in the Arena Podcast

In 2022 we became the #1 podcast for Christian men on Spotify. It is our fastest-growing audience with the widest global reach at 168 nations so far. Join me as I interview experts and authors about various subjects related to Biblical masculinity.

A-Game

The men of your team are watching you. They notice the scribbled pages in your workbook where you took copious notes when you were a team member. They also notice the blank pages where you were unprepared. Don't wing it. Collect your thoughts before every team meeting. Bring your A-Game. Come prepared with personal notes written in this Playbook. Men aren't dumb. They know when you come unprepared, and you send the wrong message. Please bring your A-Game.

Carry Equal Loads

Are you a co-team leader? If so, have you carried enough weight to earn the respect of your fellow team members? Or have you deferred the burden of leadership to your co-captain? Share the load during all team meetings. Make sure team meetings represent both captains equally every week. We recommend that when one man teaches the lesson the other runs and controls the meeting.

Finger on the Pulse

Each team has a unique identity. The morale of the men is at different levels. What is the heartbeat of your men? Who's been missing? Who seems disengaged? Are you connecting with your co-leader?

Half Full Glass

When you coach, make sure to be positive. The negative will be easier to spot but be careful to acknowledge more positive than negative. It will pay dividends in the end.

75% Mandatory Attendance

Don't take roll or keep score but notice if men don't seem committed. Your group will only be as committed as your least-committed team member. While we are at it, your men will only be as committed to attending as you are. Remember you are the example.

Follow Us

Make sure you follow our moving on most social media outlets @themeninthearena or @meninthearena. Join the Men in the Arena Facebook group with thousands of other men seeking their best version in Christ just like you.

Quarterly Events

You are only responsible for your team, but you are responsible to them. These are your guys. Their marriages are your marriages. Their children are your children. Continue to bond with your team members and maintain relationships with them. We recommend one event per season: winter, spring summer, and fall.

Intergenerational vs. Multigenerational

Where multigenerational groups are age-specific, we are an intergenerational ministry. This means we integrate the men into the same groups whenever possible. Work hard to include men from as many decades of life as possible. This will play in your favor in several ways. First, the younger men will inspire the older guys with their raw and unrefined passion. As we age the fires of skepticism replace the dreams of our youth. Younger men help curtail this in the older ones. Second, the older men will exponentially propel the younger ones with their wisdom and experience. They bring a lifetime of experience that the younger ones haven't had a chance to encounter yet. Too much of either youth or age can hamper a team's effectiveness You need both. This is what it means to be intergenerational.

Five Hours

Plan on spending five hours a week as a team leader. That includes contacting the men, preparing the weekly meeting, personal visits, counseling, etc. Set a goal of meeting with one man from your group every other week. Summers are also a great time to have a group potluck with the men and their wives.

Family Time
Make your team meeting feel more like family time than work time. It's not the place for them to perform but to relax, enjoy fellowship, and receive support from other brothers.

Airtime
Make sure every man gets a chance to share every week. It's your job as a leader to make sure every man is an equal opportunity to participate every week.

Floor Stare
Most of us struggle when we ask a question and get blank stares and hear crickets. As we grow more comfortable leading a Bible study, the tendency is to talk more. Better leaders talk less and master the art of question-asking and response. Try this. The next time you ask an open-ended question (which should be every time), stare at the floor or your notebook until guys begin to answer. Let them deal with the awkward silence and figure out an answer.

Summers Question
On a recent Men in the Arena Facebook forum, a question was raised about why men's groups stopped meeting for the summer. We don't mandate that groups stop meeting but highly recommend taking a break from June until September. There are three primary reasons for this: 1) People are gone during summer and group attendance is often low and inconsistent, 2) groups are led by volunteers who need a break, and 3) groups that meet through the summer historically fall victim to attrition at a much higher rate than those who don't.

Safe Place
A team is many things, including a hospital for broken men. Don't put pressure to conform to certain behaviors. Instead, show men the love of Jesus. Live by the creed, "Long-term, low pressure." Make your meetings a confidential place and allow men to run in their lane (unless there is an unrepeated sin) at their pace.

If You Don't Say It, They Won't Do It
Make sure your men know beyond the shadow of a doubt what commitment level you expect from them. If they miss more than 25% of the meetings, they will hurt the dynamics of your team and will not get much out of their time with you. Attendance should be no less than 75% of the time. Your goal is to equip future team leaders not sporadic attendees so hold them to a high standard.

Communication is Key

Make sure to communicate to the men on your team at least 48 hours before your meeting (text, e-mail, direct message, etc.) to remind them about the weekly meeting so they can come prepared. Make sure you train the men on your team to communicate back each week, especially if they will not be able to attend. Leaders should know who will be in attendance every week.

They are Watching

Your guys are watching you. They're watching how you live, love, serve, and run your Men in the Arena team. Your goal is to legacy with these men. Legacy happens when your fellow team members become Arena leaders like yourself, but you must lead them by your example.

Start New Teams

Your goal is to disciple your men to the point where they are willing and able to step out on faith and start a new team. Take the time to ask your men to start their team. The time will come when you must ask each of your men to, pair up, step out in faith, and start a group of their own.

Draw Out

Draw out the quiet man without making him feel violated, disrespected, or uncomfortable. Get a sense of his pace and timing. If he isn't ready to talk, don't try to force him. Privately ask a man who talks a lot to help you draw out the other man.

Champion

The Apostle Paul "Even when I was in Thessalonica you sent help more than once. I don't say this because I want a gift from you. Rather, I want you to receive a reward for your kindness. (Philippians 4:16-17)" If this ministry has impacted your life consider joining us receiving further eternal dividends by becoming a financial champion, and helping other men have a Hero Story to tell!

THE MEN'S MINISTRY PLAYBOOK

YOUR CLOSER: GREAT "AND ONE" QUESTIONS

If you have some time to spare, want to mix it up a bit, or want to take a deep time not the lives of your men, these questions are designed to mine out the depth of a man's heart.

God's Woman
1. How strong are the guardrails in how you interact with another woman?
2. Are you tempted to breach (or have you) a guardrail since we met last?
3. How are you treating your wife? Did she get mad at you this week?
4. Which one of your wedding vows did you violate this week?
5. How are you doing in your battle against lust?

God's Word
1. How many days since we last met were you in the Word?
2. What is God teaching you through the Word?
3. How are you doing with obedience? Are you doing what He is teaching you to do?
4. What part of God's Word are you wrestling3 with this week?
5. What nugget are you taking away from today's meeting?

God's Will
1. What is God saying to you this week?
2. What is God telling you to do?
3. What were you made for?
4. Talk about your spiritual SHAPE…
5. Where have you rebelled against God's will this week?

God's Work
1. Where are you serving outside of biblical mandates (wife, children, etc.)?
2. What is your biggest work struggle?
3. Who is your biggest work struggle?
4. Have you cheated, stolen, or lied at work this week?
5. Have you robbed your employer because of laziness or wasting time on personal stuff?

God's Wampum
1. How are you spending your time, your talents, and your money?
2. Have you robbed God in any area this week?
3. Who owns you through debt and what are you doing to get out of it?
4. Did you tithe 10% off your last paycheck?
5. What Kingdom causes do you invest in?

God's Witness
1. Who are you witnessing to, sharing the gospel with, and ministering to?
2. What kind of witness were you at work and home this week?
3. In whose eyes is your witness hindered because of your words or actions?
4. Who might be surprised if I told them that you were a follower of Jesus?
5. Where did you bring Jesus up in conversation this week?

SECTION II: YOUR MEETINGS

BEFORE YOU START: HOW TO USE THIS BOOK

Select one man in your group to open in prayer.

Open up the room for men to share a story of how God changed them, used them to impact someone else, or share about someone they love who has been deeply impacted by God.

Prep men ahead-of-time to share no more than 10 minutes of their story, including their past, their spiritual journey, and current events. Skip the Round Table Question until all men have shared their personal story.

This is not your time to pontificate, but a time to facilitate discussion.

NINE TRAITS OF MANHOOD SERIES

TEAM MEETING 1
"REMEMBER YOUR PAST"

OPENING PRAYER (5 MINS)

HERO STORIES (5 MINS)

PERSONAL STORY/ROUND TABLE QUESTION (10 MINS)
Each man will share his story—one man per week—until all men have shared. Once all the men have shared their personal stories, have every man at your team meeting answer a "Round Table Question" relating to the topic for the day.

Round Table Question: What family stories are you passing on to your children?

WEEKLY STUDY (30 MINS)
Take turns reading as Job reflects on the "good ole days" in Job 29:1-25.

What's the Biblical tension when it comes to remembering our past?
Philippians 3:13-14, and Isaiah 43:18-19
NOTES:

"God would not bring you through the Red Sea and turn around and allow you to perish in a fish pond."
~Johnnie Dent Jr.

Men's Ministry Playbook - Page 50

TEAM MEETINGS: HOW TO USE THIS BOOK

NINE TRAITS OF MANHOOD SERIES
TEAM MEETING 1 (CONT'D)

What should every man remember?

His life before Jesus. Acts 26:4-12, Ephesians 2:11-12, and Philippians 3:4-7

His God. Ecclesiastes 12:1, 2 Timothy 2:8, and Luke 22:19

The Word of God. John 15:20, Jude 1:17, 2 Peter 1:19-21, and Psalm 119:9-11

Spiritual victories. Romans 1:8, Philippians 1:3, 1 Thessalonians 1:2-7, and 1 Samuel 17:34-36

Wise advice. 2 Corinthians 9:6, 2 Thessalonians 2:5, Philippians 4:9, and Hebrews 13:7

His protégé. 2 Timothy 1:3, and Philemon 1:4

The white-hot fire of salvation. Hebrews 10:32, and Revelation 2:4-5

HUDDLE TIME (15 MINS)
Question of the week: Where are you lost in your story?
Pray for Each Other

NOTES:

> Bold sections are the questions or statements to discuss. Anything not in bold is to read on your own or look up in Scripture.

> The most effective way to lead is to ask the question in bold, then have men look up one Scripture at a time and answer how it relates to the question asked.

> If your group is larger than 10, it is highly effective to break up into huddles of 3-5 to pray together, answer a "And One" question, and end your meeting.

NINE TRAITS OF MANHOOD SERIES

TEAM MEETING 1
"REMEMBER YOUR PAST"

OPENING PRAYER (5 MINS)

HERO STORIES (5 MINS)

PERSONAL STORY/ROUND TABLE QUESTION (10 MINS)
Each man will share his story—one man per week—until all men have shared. Once all the men have shared their personal stories, have every man answer a "Round Table Question" relating to the topic for the day.

Round Table Question: What family stories are you passing on to your children?

WEEKLY STUDY (30 MINS)
Take turns reading as Job reflects on the "good ole days" in Job 29:1-25.

What's the Biblical tension when it comes to remembering our past?
Philippians 3:13-14, and Isaiah 43:18-19

NOTES:

"God would not bring you through the Red Sea and turn around and allow you to perish in a fish pond." ~Johnnie Dent Jr.

NINE TRAITS OF MANHOOD SERIES
TEAM MEETING 1 (CONT'D)

What should every man remember?

His life before Jesus. Acts 26:4-12, Ephesians 2:11-12, and Philippians 3:4-7

His God. Ecclesiastes 12:1, 2 Timothy 2:8, and Luke 22:19

The Word of God. John 15:20, Jude 1:17, 2 Peter 1:19-21, and Psalm 119:9-11

Spiritual victories. Romans 1:8, Philippians 1:3, 1 Thessalonians1:2-7, and 1 Samuel 17:34-36

Wise advice. 2 Corinthians 9:6, 2 Thessalonians 2:5, Philippians 4:9, and Hebrews 13:7

His protégé. 2 Timothy1:3, and Philemon 1:4

The white-hot fire of salvation. Hebrews 10:32, and Revelation 2:4-5

HUDDLE TIME (15 MINS)
Question of the week: Where are you lost in your story?
"And One" Question
Pray for Each Other

NOTES:

"Men will never fully recapture their missing manhood until they repent of modern arrogance and humbly look at the history of American masculinity to see what truths it has to pass on to them. Each man's past and the histories of others are wonderful instructors. Men isolate themselves from the past at great peril. They are not islands. All of the male history is their history. "
~Weldon Hardenbrook, *Missing from Action*

NINE TRAITS OF MANHOOD SERIES

TEAM MEETING 2
"A MAN STAYS CLOSE TO HIS KIDS"

OPENING PRAYER (5 MINS)

HERO STORIES (5 MINS)

PERSONAL STORY/ROUND TABLE QUESTION (10 MINS)
Each man will share his story—one man per week—until all men have shared. Once all the men have shared their personal stories, have every man answer a "Round Table Question" relating to the topic for the day.

Round Table Question: Which of your kids is a challenge right now?

WEEKLY STUDY (30 MINS)
Read the story of Job losing his children in Job 1:18-21.

"Naked I came from my mother's womb, and naked I will depart. The Lord gave and the Lord has taken away; may the name of the Lord be praised." ~Job, 1:21

What might Job have meant by "my children were around me"?

NOTES:

"A child who is allowed to be disrespectful to his parents will not have true respect for anyone." ~Billy Graham

NINE TRAITS OF MANHOOD SERIES
TEAM MEETING 2 (CONT'D)

How do the following Psalms and Proverbs help a man stay close to his children? Psalm 37:25-26, 78:5-6 127:3-5, Proverbs 13:22, 14:26, and 14:20

What does the Apostle Paul teach in the following Epistles about fathering? Ephesians 6:1-4, Colossians 3:20-21, 1 Timothy 3:4, 12, and Titus 1:6

What is the greatest temptation pulling men away from their children? Galatians 6:9

"...when the Almighty was still with me, and my children were around me..." ~Job, 29:5

How do you stay engaged with your children after a long day of work?

Discuss a plan to remain engaged with your family from 6:00 - 9:00 p.m.

"When you come home from work, your real job begins. You will be remembered by those who love you the most in large part by what you did after work. What you put to the grindstone in life will be what is remembered on your tombstone. Choose wisely." ~Jim Ramos

HUDDLE TIME (15 MINS)
Question of the week: How can you reconnect with your child's heart?
"And One" Question
Pray for Each Other

NOTES:

"We never know the love of a parent till we become one ourselves." ~Henry Ward Beecher

NINE TRAITS OF MANHOOD SERIES

TEAM MEETING 3 "FATHER TO THE FATHERLESS"

OPENING PRAYER (5 MINS)

HERO STORIES (5 MINS)

PERSONAL STORY/ROUND TABLE QUESTION (10 MINS)
Each man will share his story—one man per week—until all men have shared. Once all the men have shared their personal stories, have every man answer a "Round Table Question" relating to the topic for the day.

Round Table Question: What's your experience with fatherlessness?

WEEKLY STUDY (30 MINS)
"Whoever heard me spoke well of me, and those who saw me commended me because I rescued the poor who cried for help, and the fatherless who had none to assist him." ~Job, 29:11-12

What do the following verses teach us about a man's role in the lives of children who do not have an engaged father figure?
Job 29:11-12, 31:16-17, and 21-22

NOTES:

"Injustice anywhere is a threat to justice everywhere." ~Martin Luther King Jr.

NINE TRAITS OF MANHOOD SERIES
TEAM MEETING 3 (CONT'D)

Who are the fatherless of our culture?

Fatherless is mentioned 39 times in the Bible and orphan(s) is mentioned 5 times.

God defends the fatherless. Deuteronomy 10:17-18, Psalm 10:18, and 82:3

God takes care of the fatherless. Deuteronomy 14:28-29, Psalm 10:14, 146:9, and Proverbs 23:10-11

God's mandate is to care for the fatherless. Deuteronomy 24:17-22

God is a father to the fatherless. Psalm 68:5

Man's mandate to do the same is Isaiah. 1:15-17 and 10:1-2

Jesus' promise to parent us. John 14:18-19

What is a practical response to James 1:27?

"Religion that God our Father accepts as pure and faultless is this: to look after orphans and widows in their distress and to keep oneself from being polluted by the world." ~James, 1:27

HUDDLE TIME (15 MINS)
Question of the week: What "fatherless" children are you reaching out to?
"And One" Question. Pray for Each Other

NOTES:

"24 million children will go to bed without a biological father in the home, 66% are not expected to live with their father through age 18, and every third child is born out of wedlock."
~The U.S. Census Bureau (2001)

"Half of all children from divorce will not see their father for over a year. Children in fatherless homes are 5 times more likely to live in poverty, have emotional problems, and repeat a grade in school."
~The American Academy of Pediatrics (2003)

NINE TRAITS OF MANHOOD SERIES

TEAM MEETING 4 "ENFORCER OF JUSTICE"

OPENING PRAYER (5 MINS)

HERO STORIES (5 MINS)

PERSONAL STORY/ROUND TABLE QUESTION (10 MINS)
Each man will share his personal story—one man per week—until all men have shared. Then use this time to answer the "Round Table Question."

Round Table Question: What injustices in the world bother you?

WEEKLY STUDY (30 MINS)
"I put on righteousness as my clothing; justice was my robe and my turban. I was eyes to the blind and feet to the lame. I was a father to the needy; I took up the case of the stranger. I broke the fangs of the wicked and snatched the victims from their teeth." ~Job, 29:14-17

Define God's justice. Deuteronomy 16:19, 24:17, 1 Samuel 8:3, 1 Kings 3:11, Job 19:7, and Proverbs 18:5, 29:4.

Why has culture trained men to feel guilty for something innately masculine: fighting against injustice?

NOTES:

"The superior man...stands erect bending above the fallen. He rises by lifting others."
~Robert Green Ingersoll

NINE TRAITS OF MANHOOD SERIES
TEAM MEETING 4 (CONT'D)

According to Job 29:14, what is needed to enforce justice? Proverbs 21:15, 28:5, and Ephesians 6:14

> *"Beyond all his other character traits, Job was first and foremost, a pursuer of God. The pursuit of God is a mark of a real man."*
> ~Weldon Hardenbrook, *Missing from Action*

How does Jesus model the masculine sense of enforcer of justice? Mark 10:13-15 and John 2:13-17 (Psalm 69:9)

Where should we draw the line when enforcing justice? Ephesians 4:26-27, 29-31, 1 Timothy 2:8, and James 1:19-20

> *"In my life, as in football, I choose to be a warrior, not a spectator. I'm a warrior against hate and ignorance, poverty, and injustice. I'm a warrior for God and the gospel of Jesus Christ. Life is warfare, and no warfare is more intense than spiritual warfare."* ~Pat Williams, *The Warrior Within*

What four groups of people is Job 29 talking about in verses 15-16? Identify who is part of each of these four groups.
1. "Eyes to the Blind" (15)
2. "Feet to the lame" (15)
3. "Father to the needy" (16)
4. "Took up the case of the stranger" (16)

What do the four groups in verses 15-16 have in common? If Job lived in our time and location, what other groups might he have mentioned? Verse 17 epitomizes justice in the real world. **What does it look like?**

How is justice different than revenge? Leviticus 19:18 and Romans 12:17-21

HUDDLE TIME (15 MINS)
Question of the week: What "fatherless" children are you reaching out to?
"And One" Question. Pray for Each Other

> *"Hostile charges against men's natural inclination to aggressively seek justice involve a play on feminized emotions. They are a sneaky, disarming attempt to strip males of their manhood-to make them feel guilty over something innately masculine. Real men get angry over injustice. Therefore, today's men must resist guilt for thinking, acting, and feeling the way real men think, act, and feel."*
> ~Weldon Hardenbrook, *Missing from Action*

NINE TRAITS OF MANHOOD SERIES

TEAM MEETING 5 "GODLY COMPASSION"

OPENING PRAYER (5 MINS)

HERO STORIES (5 MINS)

PERSONAL STORY/ROUND TABLE QUESTION (10 MINS)
Each man will share his personal story—one man per week—until all men have shared. Then use this time to answer the "Round Table Question."

Round Table Question: Who do you feel the most compassion for?

WEEKLY STUDY (30 MINS)
What does compassion look like?

> *"Because I rescued the poor who cried for help, and the fatherless who had none to assist him. The man who was dying blessed me; I made the widow's heart sing."*
> ~Job, 29:12-13

"Compassion: A feeling of deep sympathy and sorrow for another who is stricken by misfortune, accompanied by a strong desire to alleviate the suffering. Definition of Compassion from answers.com The Hebrew (*hamal*, *rachuwm*) and Greek (*splanchnisomai*) words sometimes translated as 'compassion' also bear a broader meanings such as 'to show pity,' 'to love,' and 'to show mercy.'" ~Biblestudytools.com

NOTES:

NINE TRAITS OF MANHOOD SERIES
TEAM MEETING 5 (CONT'D)

What are the four categories of humanity listed in Job 29:12-13?

Discuss each of the four.
1. the poor who cried for help (12)
2. the fatherless who had no one to assist him (12)
3. the man who was dying (13)
4. the widows (13)

What does verse 12 add that verse 13 does not? When does compassion become enabling? Check out the compassion of Jesus. What stirs Jesus' compassion in here? Matthew 9:36-38, 14:14, 20:34, and Mark 6:34.

How should our hearts be similarly stirred?

"Compassion is sometimes the fatal capacity for feeling what it is like to be inside of somebody else's skin. It is the knowledge that there can never really be any peace and joy for me until there is peace and joy finally for you." ~Fredrick Buechner

Study the Good Samaritan Story in Luke 10:30-37. What do you discover about compassion?

"The road from Jerusalem to Jericho was notoriously dangerous. Jerusalem is 2,300 feet above sea level; the Dead Sea, near which Jericho stood, is 1,300 feet below sea level. So then, in somewhat less than twenty miles, this road dropped 3,600 feet. It was a road of narrow, rocky passages, and sudden turns which made it the happy hunting ground for brigands. In the fifth century, Jerome tells us that it was still called "The Bloody Way." ~William Barclay's Commentary

Where is the balance between compassion and accountability for one's actions?

The morals of the universe bend at the elbow of justice.
~Martin Luther King Jr.

HUDDLE TIME (15 MINS)
Question of the week: What breaks your heart? What are you doing about it?
"And One" Question. Pray for Each Other.

> Today's men talk about helping the poor. But from my observation, the ones who strike the loudest cymbals to harangue the rich into giving to the poor usually never leave their academic environments to do the work themselves. Others, because of their laziness, have never acquired enough to have something to give anyway. Both talk the talk but don't bring mercy into reality by offering a flesh-and-blood hand to a single impoverished soul who bears a personal name."
> ~Weldon Hardenbrook, *Missing from Action*

NINE TRAITS OF MANHOOD SERIES

TEAM MEETING 6
"A MAN RESPECTED"

OPENING PRAYER (5 MINS)

HERO STORIES (5 MINS)

PERSONAL STORY/ROUND TABLE QUESTION (10 MINS)
Each man will share his personal story—one man per week—until all men have shared. Then use this time to answer the "Round Table Question."

Round Table Question: What man do you most respect?

WEEKLY STUDY (30 MINS)
Where can you see honor and respect working together in Job 29:7-8?

"When I went to the gate of the city and took my seat in the public square, the young men saw me and stepped aside and the old men rose to their feet; the chief men refrained from speaking and covered their mouths with their hands; the voices of the nobles were hushed, and their tongues stuck to the roof of their mouths. Whoever heard me spoke well of me, and those who saw me commended me." ~Job, 29:7-11

NOTES:

"Loved by few, hated by many, respected by all." ~Unknown

NINE TRAITS OF MANHOOD SERIES
TEAM MEETING 6 (CONT'D)

Who is Job leading in verses 9-10? Who is listening to him? Who is "speaking well" of Job in verse 11 and what can we learn from it?

> *"Gates were the courts of Justice and Job was the supreme Magistrate."*
> ~Adam Clarke

What does the Bible teach about respecting our parents? Leviticus 19:3 and 1 Timothy 3:4

Toward our Elders? Leviticus 19:32, Lamentations 5:12, and Titus 2:2

> *"If a man does not pursue wisdom, mercy, and justice, what is there to respect? Wives are told in the Holy Scriptures to respect their husbands. But let's be honest. Who has killed their respect? Men, that's who. Men today are making it almost impossible for women to respect them. I know of large numbers of Christian women who respect and honor their husbands out of obedience to the Lord, not because of their husbands' persistent, merciful, no-nonsense holiness. Job gained the respect of others because of his true manliness, and he also had the respect of God Himself!"*
> ~Wheldon Hardenbrook, *Missing from Action*

- **Toward God?** Isaiah 5:12, Malachi 1:6
- **Toward Humanity?** 1 Peter 2:17
- **Toward Government?** Romans 13:6-7, 1 Peter 2:13-14
- **Toward Employers?** Ephesians 6:5, 1 Timothy 6:1-2, and 1 Peter 2:18
- **Toward Spiritual Authority?** 1 Thessalonians 5:12-13
- **Toward those who oppose our faith?** 1 Peter 3:15
- **Toward Spouses?** Ephesians 5:33, and 1 Peter 3:7

What does the Bible say about earning respect? Proverbs 29:23, Psalm 112:4-9, and 1 Timothy 3:2-10

What are some characteristics of Job that we should follow if we want to be respected like he was?

HUDDLE TIME (15 MINS)
Question of the week: Are you respected by others? Grade yourself A-F.
"And One" Question. Pray for Each Other

> *"If you're not being admired by other men, you're being hurt."* ~Unknown

NINE TRAITS OF MANHOOD SERIES

TEAM MEETING 7
"DEEP ROOTS IN HIS COMMUNITY"

OPENING PRAYER (5 MINS)

HERO STORIES (5 MINS)

PERSONAL STORY/ROUND TABLE QUESTION (10 MINS)
Each man will share his personal story—one man per week—until all men have shared. Then use this time to answer the "Round Table Question."

Round Table Question: How long have you lived in your current home?

WEEKLY STUDY (30 MINS)
How does Job's comment in verse 18, "I will die in my house" differ from the actions of people today?

"I thought, 'I will die in my own house, my days as numerous as the grains of sand. My roots will reach to the water, and the dew will lie all night on my branches. My glory will remain fresh in me, the bow ever new in my hand.'" ~Job, 29:18-20

NOTES:

"A big part of leadership is the ability to stick with the dream for a long time. Long enough that the critics realize you are going to get there one way or another... so they follow."
~Seth Godin, Tribes

"Storms make oaks take deeper root."
~George Herbert

NINE TRAITS OF MANHOOD SERIES
TEAM MEETING 7 (CONT'D)

How do the following verses apply to deep roots?
Mark 12:31, Romans 13:8-10, and Galatians 5:13-15

How does sinking deep roots into a community help a man bear fruit?
Psalms 1:3, Jeremiah 17:7-8, Matthew 7:16 and 20

Going back to Job 29:18-20, what does "dew will lie all night on my branches" mean in the context of sinking deep roots?

What did Job mean in verse 20 by, "My glory will remain fresh in me, the bow ever new in my hand?"

What strength does a man discover when his roots run deep?

How do his community and church benefit?

What similarities can you see between a man's "glory" and a "new bow"?
James 1:9-12

HUDDLE TIME (15 MINS)
Question of the week: How do you see your roots affecting those around you?
"And One" Question
Pray for Each Other

NOTES:

We have become a nation of strangers." ~Vance Packard

NINE TRAITS OF MANHOOD SERIES

TEAM MEETING 8
"MAN OF WISDOM"

OPENING PRAYER (5 MINS)

HERO STORIES (5 MINS)

PERSONAL STORY/ROUND TABLE QUESTION (10 MINS)
Each man will share his personal story—one man per week—until all men have shared. Then use this time to answer the "Round Table Question."

Round Table Question: Who is the wisest person you know?

WEEKLY STUDY (30 MINS)
What is wisdom?

"Men listened to me expectantly, waiting in silence for my counsel. After I had spoken, they spoke no more my words fell gently on their ears. They waited for me as for showers and drank in my words as the spring rain." ~Job, 29:21-23

Where do we find it? How do we obtain it?

NOTES:

"The only true wisdom is knowing you know nothing." ~Socrates

NINE TRAITS OF MANHOOD SERIES
TEAM MEETING 8 (CONT'D)

How does a man become wise without life experience?

What can younger men learn about wisdom from older men?

> "The true leader is not the one who speaks the most,
> but the one people look to last." ~Jim Ramos

According to verse 22, how does the man of wisdom make his point?
Colossians 4:6, Ephesians 4:15, 29, and 2 Timothy 2:24-25

Where does wisdom originate? Why do you think this is?
Proverbs 1:7, 2:6, and 30:2-3

Where should men place wisdom on your list of priorities?
Proverbs 4:7, 16:16, and 19:8

How does wisdom aid in parenting? Proverbs 24:3, and 29:15

What promise do we discover in James 1:5?

What does the Bible call a man who does not seek wisdom?
Proverbs 10:31, 12:8, 17:24, 24:7, and 28:26

HUDDLE TIME (15 MINS)
Question of the week: Where have you acted foolish this week?
What happened?
"And One" Question. Pray for Each Other.

NOTES:

The Law of E.F. Hutton: When the real leader speaks, people listen.
~John Maxwell, *The 21 Irrefutable Laws of Leadership*

NINE TRAITS OF MANHOOD SERIES

TEAM MEETING 9
"GODHUNTER"

OPENING PRAYER (5 MINS)

HERO STORIES (5 MINS)

PERSONAL STORY/ROUND TABLE QUESTION (10 MINS)
Each man will share his personal story—one man per week—until all men have shared. Then use this time to answer the "Round Table Question."

Round Table Question: What does your schedule show you pursue hardest in your life?

WEEKLY STUDY (30 MINS)
"How I long for the months gone by, for the days when God watched over me when his lamp shone upon my head and by his light I walked through darkness! Oh, for the days when I was in my prime when God's intimate friendship blessed my house." ~Job, 29:2-4

What can you gather about Job's relationship with God? Can you think of a verse to support your answer? (For example, verse 3: "By his light, I walked through darkness." Support Verse: Psalm 119:105)

NOTES:

"We can say with confidence that we have never known a man whose life has changed in any significant way apart from the regular study of God's Word."
~Patrick Morley, David Delk, and Brett Clemmer, *No Man Left Behind*

NINE TRAITS OF MANHOOD SERIES
TEAM MEETING 9 (CONT'D)

What did God have to say about His relationship with Job? Job 1:4-8

What is Philippians 3:12-14 all about?

"The Greek word dioko, literally means 'I pursue.' It is translated in Philippians 3 as 'press on.' Dioko is a hunting word and it is also used in foot-racing. It is a strong expression of active and earnest endeavor. It is correlative with 'take hold' in several passages in the sense of 'pursue and overtake,' 'chase and capture.'"
~Tyndale New Testament Commentaries

"The impulse to pursue God originates with God, but the outworking of that impulse is our following hard after Him. All the time we are pursuing Him we are already in His hand."
~A.W. Tozer, The Pursuit of God

"...so that he might sanctify her, having cleansed her by the washing of water with the word."
~Ephesians 5:26 NASB

Compare Philippians 3:8 with 3:13. What do you see about pursuing God?

"Skubala is the Greek word for dung or rubbish. In common language, it was used to mean "that which is thrown to the dogs." In medical language, it means 'excrement or dung.'"
~William Barclay Commentary

What does Paul mean in Philippians 3:12 and 14 when he says, "I press on"?

What does "I want to know Christ" mean to you? How do you seek to know him better?

Job had an "intimate friendship" (verse 4) with God. What does your relationship with God look like?

HUDDLE TIME (15 MINS)
Question of the week: What can you do to know Christ more?
"And One" Question. Pray for Each Other

"If knowing Christ is experiencing him through a personal relationship, then what does that look like for a man of God?" ~Kenneth S. Wuest, *Word Studies in the Greek New Testament*

DEALING WITH P.M.S. (PASSIVE MALE SYNDROME)

TEAM MEETING 10
"THE FALL"

OPENING PRAYER (5 MINS)

HERO STORIES (5 MINS)

PERSONAL STORY (10 MINS)
Each man will share his personal story—one man per week—until all men have shared. Then use this time to answer the "Round Table Question."

Round Table Question: When do you find it hardest to stay engaged with your family?

WEEKLY STUDY (30 MINS)
Read Genesis 3:1-19, appropriately titled "The Fall."

Where was Adam during the discourse between Eve and the Serpent? What do you think he was doing?

Look at Adam in Genesis 3:6-7, 12, and 17-19.
What happened to him?

NOTES:

DEALING WITH P.M.S. (PASSIVE MALE SYNDROME)
TEAM MEETING 10 (CONT'D)

Some possible reasons why Satan spoke to Eve and not to Adam. Which one do you prefer and why?

1. Satan knew he could not engage Adam in a war of words. (Guys use an average of 7 to 10 thousand words a day, but women use from 15 to 30 thousand.)

2. Men tend to be literal in their interpretations of words. Women tend to be interpretive.

3. While present when Eve eats the fruit, Adam may not have been around for the dialogue with Satan.

4. Adam may have been too busy staring at Eve's naked body to hear the dialogue between Eve and the Serpent!

5. God's authority was on Adam (not on Eve) and Satan loves causing division and confusion.

Being "more crafty than any beast," why did Satan approach Eve instead of Adam (Genesis 3:1)?

NOTES:

DEALING WITH P.M.S. (PASSIVE MALE SYNDROME)
TEAM MEETING 10 (CONT'D)

"The ordinary man is passive...against major events, he is as helpless as against the elements. So far from endeavoring to influence the future, he simply lies down and lets things happen to him."
~George Orwell

How might Adam have responded differently to the temptation than Eve?

Who is to blame in the Garden? Who does the LORD God hold (Genesis 3:1-19) fundamentally responsible for the catastrophic sin, Adam or Eve?
Romans 5:14, and 1 Corinthians 15:21-22

What about Eve? 1 Timothy 2:14

NOTES:

"As naturally aggressive as Adam was, when the moment of authentic manhood arrived—when he was called upon to act responsibly, take charge spiritually, and protect his woman—Adam just stood there! He went flat. He became passive. He refused to accept the social and spiritual responsibilities entrusted to him by God. Men have been imitating Adam ever since. Real manhood begins with a decision to reject social and spiritual passivity."
~Robert Lewis, *Raising a Modern Day Knight*

DEALING WITH P.M.S. (PASSIVE MALE SYNDROME)
TEAM MEETING 10 (CONT'D)

"I'm convinced, after counseling hundreds of couples for more than two decades, that a major factor in the failure of marriages is the passivity of men."
~Bill Perkins, *Six Battles Every Man Must Win*

What are some consequences of PMS (Passive Male Syndrome)?
Genesis 3:21-24, Romans 5:8, 12, 15, and 6:23

The consequence of sin is death. God killed an animal to cover Adam and Eve's sins (Genesis 3:21). He sent his son Jesus to cover ours (1 Peter 3:18).

HUDDLE TIME (10 MINS)
Question of the week: Where are you the most passive?
"And One" Question
Pray for Each Other

NOTES:

"Passive men extend something that looks like grace—a disposition to be generous, helpful, and merciful. However, the reason passive men accept insults and other forms of humiliation is that they fear what might happen with an eruption of conflict—the sound of life happening."
~Paul Coughlin, No More Christian Nice Guy

DEALING WITH P.M.S. (PASSIVE MALE SYNDROME)

TEAM MEETING 11
"PASSIVE POOL"

OPENING PRAYER (5 MINS)

HERO STORIES (5 MINS)

PERSONAL STORY (10 MINS)
Each man will share his personal story—one man per week—until all men have shared. Then use this time to answer the "Round Table Question."

Round Table Question: What is stereotypical "Christian man" behavior according to our culture?

WEEKLY STUDY (30 MINS)
Take turns reading the story in John 5:1-15.

Bethesda in Aramaic means "house of mercy." How is this name symbolic of what is about to happen in this story?

NOTES:

"I wish more people would have the guts to stand against the passivity that is choking the life out of Christian men." ~Paul Coughlin, *No More Christian Nice Guy*

DEALING WITH P.M.S. (PASSIVE MALE SYNDROME)
TEAM MEETING 11 (CONT'D)

What do we learn about the character of the paralytic from verses 6-7?

Compare the responses of others needing healing in Matthew 9:27, 20:30-31, and Luke 9:38-40.

How does the invalid's answer reflect his mindset and passivity?
Deuteronomy 4:29, Matthew 7:7, and Philippians 4:6

How does Jesus respond to the passivity of this man in verses 8-9?

> "The attitude of so many Christians (men) today is anything but fierce. We're passive, acquiescent. We're acting as if the battle is over as if the world and the lamb are now fast friends."
> ~John Eldredge, *Waking the Dead*

How might Jesus respond similarly to your passivity?

NOTES:

DEALING WITH P.M.S. (PASSIVE MALE SYNDROME)
TEAM MEETING 11 (CONT'D)

"In John 5:11-12 the paralytic seems to have felt no particular gratitude to Jesus for his healing. He took no responsibility for the action on the Sabbath; and after Jesus had dealt with him the second time, he immediately informed the Jewish leaders who it was that had transgressed the Sabbath law. It seems quite unlikely that he would have been ignorant of the reason for their inquiry."
~ Expositor's Bible Commentary

In verse 14 we see Jesus' assertiveness contrasted with the invalid's passivity when we read, "He found him." Why would Jesus go to such an effort to find this man?

What does this tell you about how God feels about passivity in men?

Putting it all into the context of this man's state of mind, what do you think Jesus meant when He said to him, *"See, you are well again. Stop sinning or something worse may happen to you?"*

NOTES:

"Men, we must fight our tendency to be passive in matters about the home. The passive husband continues to be one of the most common complaints I hear from troubled homes."
Chuck Swindoll

Men's Ministry Playbook - Page 76

DEALING WITH P.M.S. (PASSIVE MALE SYNDROME)
TEAM MEETING 11 (CONT'D)

Do you think the man listened to the words of Jesus? Verses 15-16

Imagine five years from the healing. What does this man's life look like?

How does this story speak to modern man?

HUDDLE TIME (10 MINS)
Question of the week: What area(s) of your life need to be assertively "found" by you?
"And One" Question
Pray for Each Other

NOTES:

"What makes life difficult isn't that we experience pain. It's made difficult by our passivity, which undermines our willingness to fight through pain."
~Bill Perkins, *Six Battles Every Man Must Win*

GUARDRAILS SERIES

TEAM MEETING 12
"BLIND SPOTS"

OPENING PRAYER (5 MINS)

HERO STORIES (5 MINS)

ROUND TABLE QUESTION (10 MINS)
The Round Table Question is one to kick off the Bible study. It is a general question related to the day's topic, and each man gets an opportunity to share as the leader goes around the table. Thus, the Round Table Question.

Round Table Question: Do you see (forgive the pun) one potential blind spot that might haunt you if you do not deal with it today?

WEEKLY STUDY (30 MINS)
"Be on your guard; stand firm in the faith; be men of courage; be strong."
~1 Corinthians 16:13

NOTES:

"I once read that 'it is easier to raise boys than to fix men'; and I immediately recognized the simple brilliance." ~William Beausay II

GUARDRAILS SERIES
TEAM MEETING 12 (CONT'D)

What is the contrast between the plans of God and Satan for us? What other verses come to mind?
1 Peter 5:6-10

Satan "prowls around" (1 Peter 5:8) looking for strays to devour. How does isolation play a role in taking men out?

If you were Satan, who would you seek to devour first in your family, and why?
John 10:10

What schemes does Satan employ against the man of God? Job 1:9-11, 2 Corinthians 2:11, 11:3-4, 1 Thessalonians 2:18, and 2 Thessalonians 2:9-10

Every man has a blind spot. The secret is finding men with enough guts to confront it before being blindsided.

NOTES:

GUARDRAILS SERIES
TEAM MEETING 12 (CONT'D)

Satan desires one of three things from godly men according to John 10:10a. **What are they and what does each mean?**

Discuss the dangers of a blind spot.

Growing up, we loved to fish for halibut. We attached a live anchovy through the nose and dropped it to the bottom. The halibut would attack the bait from the back and slowly inhale it. When we'd get a strike, Dad would tell us to let it run and give it time to think it was safe. After giving some line, we jerked it and hooked the unsuspecting fish.

"It does not do to leave a dragon out of your calculations if you live near him."
~J.R.R. Tolkien

NOTES:

GUARDRAILS SERIES
TEAM MEETING 12 (CONT'D)

Three Potential Blind Spots:

Blind spot 1: Living above reproach.
1 Timothy 3:2, and Revelation 12:10-11

Blind spot 2: Living a Blameless Life.
Philippians 1:10, 2:14-15, 1 Thessalonians 2:10-11, and Titus 1:6-9

Blind spot 3: Living without secrets.
1 John 1:8-10, Proverbs 28:13, and James 5:16

HUDDLE TIME (10 MINS)
Question of the week: Do you have a blind spot that Satan could exploit?
"And One" Question
Pray for Each Other

NOTES:

*"Manhood is something a man earns.
One deed at a time, one task at a time, one interaction at a time."*
~David Murrow

GUARDRAILS SERIES

TEAM MEETING 13
"MARGINS"

OPENING PRAYER (5 MINS)

HERO STORIES (5 MINS)

ROUND TABLE QUESTION (10 MINS)
The Round Table Question is one to kick off the Bible study. It is a general question related to the day's topic, and each man gets an opportunity to share as the leader goes around the table. Thus, the Round Table Question.

Round Table Question: Where does your life lack margin?

WEEKLY STUDY (30 MINS)
What did you think when you saw the title of today's team meeting?

"And Jesus grew in wisdom and stature, and in favor with God and men."
~Luke, 2:52

What is the margin? Why do margins exist when writing?
NOTES:

GUARDRAILS SERIES
TEAM MEETING 13 (CONT'D)

"You're going to have to get in shape in every sense of the word. Too many men have developed a spiritual beer gut from lazy habits of life."
~Ray Pritchard, Man of Honor

How does the idea of margins relate to where you are in life?

Margins for growing in wisdom.　　　　　*"And Jesus grew in wisdom..."*

Wisdom is a promise from God.
James 1:5

Wisdom is having the ability to make the right choices based on the knowledge one possesses.

Where can you carve out margins to gain knowledge and wisdom?

Margins for growing in physical health.　　*"And Jesus grew...in stature..."*

NOTES:

GUARDRAILS SERIES
TEAM MEETING 13 (CONT'D)

How does the Bible address physical margins?
Genesis 2:2 and Hebrews 4:4

What value is there for sedentary post-industrial revolution man to get exercise?
1 Timothy 4:8

How important is it to make healthy choices about eating and drinking?
Daniel 1:8-16

Where can you carve out margins for physical fitness?

"The largest room in the world is the room for improvement."
~Harvey Mackay

Margins for spiritual growth.   *"And Jesus grew...in favor with God..."*

Can you think of any ways to grow spiritually?

1. Prayer: Petition, silence, solitude, meditation
2. Bible: Study, reading, memory, meditation
3. Church: Worship, fellowship, discipleship
4. Fellowship
5. Christian Service
6. Stewardship: Time, resources, money, talents
7. Books on spiritual growth
8. Fasting

Where do you need to carve out margins for spiritual growth?

NOTES:

GUARDRAILS SERIES
TEAM MEETING 13 (CONT'D)

Margins for social growth. *"And Jesus grew...in favor with...men."*

What does the Bible have to say about our social life?
Hebrews 10:24-25, John 13:34, Proverbs 13:20 and 27:17, and James 5:16

How does isolation put a man in danger? 1 Peter 5:8.

Where do you need to carve out time to grow in your relationships with others?

> *"Life fully alive looks busy but there is a difference between being busy and being full."* ~Anonymous

HUDDLE TIME (10 MINS)
Question of the week: What is one area you are going to carve out margin this week?
"And One" Question
Pray for Each Other

NOTES:

> *"You can't sleep late and lounge around like a couch potato if you want to win the prize of a godly life."* ~Ray Pritchard, Man of Honor

GUARDRAILS SERIES
TEAM MEETING 14
"STEWARDSHIP"

OPENING PRAYER (5 MINS)

HERO STORIES (5 MINS)

ROUND TABLE QUESTION (10 MINS)
The Round Table Question is one to kick off the Bible study. It is a general question related to the day's topic, and each man gets an opportunity to share as the leader goes around the table. Thus, the Round Table Question.

Round Table Question: How do stewardship, money, and giving relate? How are they similar?

Stewardship relates to how we manage our time, talents, physical resources, and money for the glory of God.

WEEKLY STUDY (30 MINS)
How can a man build guardrails around his RESOURCES?
Proverbs 22:7, Matthew 6:19-21, and Romans 13:8
NOTES:

"We must eat just enough to keep us fit, and a little less than will keep us fat." ~E. Stanley Jones

GUARDRAILS SERIES
TEAM MEETING 14 (CONT'D)

Here is a list of stewardship scriptures in the Bible (NIV):

Tithe: 27	Generosity: 12	Offering: 689
Tenth: 70	Money: 123	Giving: 1,727

How do you interpret these numbers?

How do you determine who will be the recipients of your generosity?

How can a man build guardrails around his TIME?
Proverbs 20:4, Ephesians 5:15-16 and Ecclesiastes 3:1-8

How can a man build guardrails around his RESOURCES?
Luke 16:1-10, 18:22, and Acts 2:44

How can a man build guardrails around his TALENTS?
Exodus 31:1-6, Acts 11:29, Romans 12:6-8, and 1 Corinthians 12:18

Why would resources and possessions be a guardrail to protect?
2 Corinthians 9:6-8 and Ephesians 4:28

"If you live like no one else, one day you will live like no one else." ~Dave Ramsey

HUDDLE TIME (10 MINS)
Question of the week: What's your stewardship "Achilles Heel"?
"And One" Question
Pray for Each Other

NOTES:

"If you are to live abundantly you must be disciplined at the pace of your eating." ~E. Stanley Jones

GUARDRAILS SERIES

TEAM MEETING 15
"THE QUIVER"

OPENING PRAYER (5 MINS)

HERO STORIES (5 MINS)

ROUND TABLE QUESTION (10 MINS)
What specific thing do you, as a father, need to protect your children against?

WEEKLY STUDY (30 MINS)
"Like arrows in the hands of a warrior are children born in one's youth. Blessed is the man whose quiver is full of them." ~Psalm 127:4-5a

Leaders are mandated in Scripture to manage their children.
1 Timothy 3:4 and 12, and Titus 1:6

What does the Bible warn against those who do not build guardrails around their children? Exodus 20:5, 34:7, and Jeremiah 2:9

What is required of the godly man? Proverbs 22:6-7, Ephesians 6:4, and Colossians 3:20-21

NOTES:

"You'll pay a very high price for doing nothing for your boy." ~William Beausay II

GUARDRAILS SERIES
TEAM MEETING 15 (CONT'D)

What is the difference between encouraging, comforting, and urging?
1 Thessalonians 2:11-12?

What guardrail does Proverbs 17:6 offer for those raising a family?

"For you know that we dealt with each of you as a father deals with his children, encouraging, comforting, and urging you to live lives worthy of God, who calls you into his kingdom and glory." ~1 Thessalonians 2:11-12

"After Mother Teresa was awarded the Nobel Peace Prize, a reporter asked her, 'What can we do to help promote world peace?' She replied, 'Go home and love your family.' The best way to love your kids is to spend time with them--lots and lots of time." ~Pat Williams, *The Warrior Within*

- **The Guardrail of Encouraging.** Share some areas you encourage your child.
- **The Guardrail of Comforting.** What signs does your child show when he or she is hurting?
- **The Guardrail of Urging.** How do you handle a man who says he does not "make" his children go to church?
- **The Guardrail of Encouraging.** How can you encourage your adult children in marriage and family issues?
- **The Guardrail of Stewardship.** Why is urging your children to be good stewards so important? Psalm 103:17, and 128:6
- **The Guardrail of an Involved Grandfather.** What are some creative ways to urge your grandchildren towards spiritual growth? Proverbs 13:22, Psalm 145:4, Deuteronomy 4:9

HUDDLE TIME (10 MINS)
Question of the week: Do you need to focus more effort on one of your children right now?
"And One" Question. Pray for Each Other

"I don't pity any man who does hard work worth doing. I admire him. I pity the creature who doesn't work, at whichever end of the social scale he may regard himself as being." ~Theodore Roosevelt

GUARDRAILS SERIES

TEAM MEETING 16
"WORDS"

OPENING PRAYER (5 MINS)

HERO STORIES (5 MINS)

ROUND TABLE QUESTION (10 MINS)
What rules do you have for how to speak about people?

WEEKLY STUDY (30 MINS)
What are your thoughts about building guardrails around your words?
James 3:1-12

What examples does James use of small things that control things great and large?

What other examples can you think of?

A mirror reading (looking at the passage and wondering why it was written to a particular group) of Scripture is putting yourself in the passage and asking, "Why would the author be writing this? What was going on there?"

NOTES:

"Christian surrender means the death of complaining."
~Gary Thomas, *Seeking the Face of God*

GUARDRAILS SERIES
TEAM MEETING 16 (CONT'D)

Discuss why you think James would come back to the topic in 3:3-12.
James 1:19-20 and 26

What does James 3:6 mean by "the tongue is a fire, a world of evil among the parts of the body"?

Still, looking at verse 6, how does the tongue corrupt the whole person?
Proverbs 17:20, and Matthew 12:34-37

Explain what verse 8 means, "no man can tame the tongue."
Galatians 5:22-23, Ephesians 4:15, 4:29, and 2 Peter 1:3-7

What tension is created by reading James 3:9-11 and Matthew 7:16-20 side-by-side?

> *"What about the inactivity of your tongue? What about when you should speak up as a man but choose to remain silent?"*
> ~Brad Ranche, "The Original 15" Men in the Arena

Discuss these rules for the tongue:
1. Don't tell someone else's story.
2. Don't say something about someone else if they aren't around to defend themselves.
3. Make sure you can always look a person in the eye after you've spoken about them.

What other rules do you have for your words?

HUDDLE TIME (10 MINS)
Question of the week: Whose story have you been telling without their permission?
"And One" Question. Pray for Each Other

NOTES:

"Freedom is just Chaos, with better lighting." ~Franklin D. Roosevelt

GUARDRAILS SERIES

TEAM MEETING 17
"CONTROL"

OPENING PRAYER (5 MINS)

HERO STORIES (5 MINS)

ROUND TABLE QUESTION (10 MINS)
How do you handle your impulses?

To many, total abstinence is easier than perfect moderation. ~Saint Augustine

WEEKLY STUDY (30 MINS)
Can someone find any Bible references for, "Everything in moderation..."?

Why is that verse so hard to find?

The test of moderation is examination. Examine your life in the following areas.

"I have found it takes a lot more discipline and maturity to live a life of moderation than total abstinence." ~Bill Perkins, *Six Battles Every Man Must Win*

NOTES:

"Nothing tastes as good as looking good feels." ~Anthony Robbins

GUARDRAILS SERIES
TEAM MEETING 17 (CONT'D)

God: Psalm 26:2, 139:23-24, Proverbs 5:21, and Jeremiah 17:10
You: 1 Corinthians 11:28 and 2 Corinthians 13:5

What has mastery over you? Romans 6:11-14, 1 Corinthians 6:12, and 2 Peter 2:18-19

Moderation is synonymous with which fruit of the Spirit?
1 Timothy 3:1-5, 2 Peter 1:5-6, and Galatians 5:22-23

Moderation is having the ability—the freedom—to say "No."
1 Corinthians 8:9-13 and Galatians 5:16-17

"Make decisions against yourself." ~Jack Hayford

What is another way to demonstrate our freedom?
Romans 14:13-18 and 2 Corinthians 6:3

Three reasons to build guardrails around our body:
1. **Sexual immorality.** 1 Corinthians 6:18-20, and 2 Timothy 2:22
2. **Alcohol.** Proverbs 20:1, 1 Corinthians 6:10, and Ephesians 5:18
3. **Diet (food and drink), Fitness, and Health.** 1 Timothy 4:8

"If you have built a tolerance to alcohol, you have a problem." ~Anonymous

Take a health class, receive prayer, join a gym, schedule an exercise regime, read a book on fitness, or simply get some help for your sin. Obesity is a sin against God and the body He gave you. Do something with your fat so you can enjoy the life God has for you.

HUDDLE TIME (10 MINS)
Question of the week: Where are you sinning against God and your body?
What are you struggling to say "no" to?
"And One" Question.. Pray for Each Other.

"Here's how you know if you drink too much. If anyone tells you, then you drink too much!"
~Andy Stanley

MAN UP SERIES

TEAM MEETING 18
"DISPLACING BLAME"

OPENING PRAYER (5 MINS)

HERO STORIES (5 MINS)

ROUND TABLE QUESTION (10 MINS)
What have you been blaming your wife for?

WEEKLY STUDY (30 MINS)
A man should accept responsibility for God's Will, God's Wampum (money), God's Work, God's Woman (and kids), God's Word, and God's Witness.

What is your gut reaction when you read Genesis 3:12?

"The man said, 'The woman you put here with me—she gave me some fruit from the tree, and I ate it.'" ~Adam, Genesis 3:12

NOTES:

"How does a man become one?"
~Patrick Morley, *No Man Left Behind*

MAN UP SERIES
TEAM MEETING 18 (CONT'D)

After The Fall of Genesis 3:9, God knew where Adam was but called for him anyway. Why did God call for Adam and not Eve?

What does this say about God's household?
Genesis 3:8-11

What is a man responsible for in his home?
Ephesians 5:22-6:4 and Colossians 3:18-21

What other passages teach us about men being responsible to lead their families?

"A man accepts responsibility..."
~Robert Lewis, *Raising of a Modern Day Knight*

Where do you see Adam manifesting in your life today?

HUDDLE TIME (10 MINS)
Question of the week: Where do you need to accept your responsibility, to lead courageously?
"And One" Question
Pray for Each Other

NOTES:

MAN UP SERIES

TEAM MEETING 19
"ACCEPT RESPONSIBILITY"

OPENING PRAYER (5 MINS)

HERO STORIES (5 MINS)

ROUND TABLE QUESTION (10 MINS)
Where does your wife want you to accept more responsibility?

WEEKLY STUDY (30 MINS)
What does it mean for a man to accept responsibility?
From Matthew 27:18-19 and 23 we learn that Pilate knew Jesus was innocent, but what happened?

What warning sign(s) can you see in a man who refuses to accept responsibility? Luke 23:3-7

Look at verse 5. Can you guess what is about to happen?

Males are the source of 90% of the world's problems. Men are the solution.

NOTES:

"A leader can give up anything except final responsibility." ~John Maxwell

MAN UP SERIES
TEAM MEETING 19 (CONT'D)

How is displacing blame a problem when men don't accept responsibility?

Men own their behaviors. Males make excuses. Males defer their responsibilities to men.

What swayed Pilate in the end? Luke 23:18-25 and Matthew 27:24

What do you learn about Pilate the man?

Where do we see men washing their hands of responsibility today? Matthew 27:24-26

Discuss how to accept responsibility in the following areas.

Spiritual Life?	Hidden Life?	Social Life?
Marriage Life?	Personal Life?	Healthy Life?
Family Life?	Church Life?	Other?

> "Life gets heavy sometimes, doesn't it? Headship is a significant responsibility. Leadership is a weighty challenge. Masculinity is no small assignment."
> ~Stu Weber, *Locking Arms*

HUDDLE TIME (10 MINS)
Question of the week: Where do you need to start leading courageously?
"And One" Question
Pray for Each Other

NOTES:

> "How can a man learn to be a man, a husband, a father, a provider, and a protector-- a full-orbed King, Warrior, Mentor, and Friend? By walking with other men who are doing it. You learn to play ball by playing ball. And masculinity is a team sport." ~Stu Weber, *Locking Arms*

LEAD FROM THE BACK SERIES

TEAM MEETING 20
"SACRIFICE"

OPENING PRAYER (5 MINS)

HERO STORIES (5 MINS)

ROUND TABLE QUESTION (10 MINS)
What comes to mind when your think of sacrifice?

WEEKLY STUDY (30 MINS)
How are sacrifice and Christianity similar?

What is the goal of spiritual leadership? Philippians 2:1-11?

Looking at Philippians 2:3 (NIV). What are "selfish ambition" and "vain conceit" and why does Paul start here? How do other translations interpret these words?

What traits do see in those who oppose the sacrificial leadership model? Philippians 1:17 and James 3:13-18

Using Philippians 2:3-4 as your guide, come up with a biblical definition for humility.

NOTES:

"Great achievement is born of great sacrifice and is never the result of selfishness." ~Napoleon Hill

LEAD FROM THE BACK SERIES
TEAM MEETING 20 (CONT'D)

"Humility is not thinking less of yourself, it is thinking of yourself, less." ~ C.S. Lewis

What are some ways can we imitate Jesus' model of sacrificial leadership?
Philippians 2:5-7

What are your thoughts on Philippians 2:7-8?
Matthew 11:28-30, 1 Peter 3:18, and John 3:16

"...but emptied Himself, taking the form of a bond-servant, and being made in the likeness of men. Being found in appearance as a man, He humbled Himself by becoming obedient to the point of death, even death on a cross."
~Apostle Paul, Philippians 2:7-8

Why do you think Paul included the exclamation "even death on a cross!"?
Deuteronomy 21:22-23, Joshua 8:29, and Galatians 3:13

"Above all, let us, as we value our self-respect, face the responsibilities with proper seriousness, courage, and high resolve." ~Theodore Roosevelt

Read Philippians 2:9-11 out loud. Have you bowed to the Name above all names, Jesus?

"God opposes the proud but gives grace to the humble." ~James 4:6-7

1. **Where have you opposed God with your foolish pride?**
2. **Have you honored Jesus' sacrifice with your life?**
3. **Do you need to receive him as Savior?**
4. **Maybe you need to step out of your arrogant self and surrender your life to Him.**

HUDDLE TIME (10 MINS)
Question of the week: What did you commit in your heart for God today?
"And One" Question. Pray for Each Other.

To give anything less than your best is to sacrifice the gift.
~Steve Prefontaine

LEAD FROM THE BACK SERIES

TEAM MEETING 21
"SERVE"

OPENING PRAYER (5 MINS)

HERO STORIES (5 MINS)

ROUND TABLE QUESTION (10 MINS)
What makes a man great?

WEEKLY STUDY (30 MINS)
"Also a dispute arose among them as to which of them was considered to be greatest. Jesus said to them, "The kings of the Gentiles lord it over them; and those who exercise authority over them call themselves Benefactors. But you are not to be like that. Instead, the greatest among you should be like the youngest, and the one who rules like the one who serves. For who is greater, the one who is at the table or the one who serves? Is it, not the one who is at the table? But I am among you as one who serves. You are those who have stood by me in my trials. And I confer on you a kingdom, just as my Father conferred one on me, so that you may eat and drink at my table in my kingdom and sit on thrones, judging the twelve tribes of Israel."
~Luke 22:24-30

What are some key characteristics of greatness?

NOTES:

"The tragedy of life is what dies inside a man while he lives." ~Albert Schweitzer

LEAD FROM THE BACK SERIES
TEAM MEETING 21 (CONT'D)

How was the Disciples' view of greatness distorted?
Mark 10:35-38 and Acts 1:6

The Disciples thought Jesus was going to overthrow the Roman Government and rule Israel. When they thought of His greatness their view was completely distorted, and based on a wrong opinion of who Jesus was and what He came to do.

"The warrior in a man is a great asset. Still, generally speaking, many wish the warrior would disappear. This is the era of the 'soft male'. Fortunately, the warrior pillar in a man just can't be voted out. It is tenacious because, rightly understood, it is part of the divine design for masculinity."
~Stu Weber, Four Pillars of a Man's Heart

Share your thoughts on this opinion:
"God has planted a seed of greatness in every man."

If the above statement is true, then why are some men so far from it? Where is the gap?

NOTES:

LEAD FROM THE BACK SERIES
TEAM MEETING 21 (CONT'D)

"Great men serve a great cause. They give themselves to something greater than themselves." ~Unknown

How is the view of greatness portrayed in culture the antithesis of the view portrayed in Scripture? How did this happen?
Luke 22:27

Secular leadership is a top-down paradigm. Spiritual leaders lead from the bottom up.

How has the polarization of spiritual and secular leadership philosophies created confusion among spiritual leaders?

In Luke 22:24 the Disciples argue over who is the greatest. Where did their idea of greatness conflict with Jesus'?
Romans 13:8, Galatians 5:13, 1 Corinthians 9:19, Matthew 20:28

When have you had a taste of Jesus-style greatness?

"God has hard-wired men for greatness. Great service. Great sacrifice. Great surrender."
~ Anonymous

NOTES:

LEAD FROM THE BACK SERIES
TEAM MEETING 21 (CONT'D)

"It is not the critic who counts: not the man who points out how the strong man stumbles or where the doer of deeds could have done better. The credit belongs to the man who is actually in the arena, whose face is marred by dust and sweat and blood, who strives valiantly, who errs and comes up short again and again, because there is no effort without error or shortcoming, but who knows the great enthusiasms, the great devotions, who spends himself for a worthy cause; who, at the best, knows, in the end, the triumph of high achievement, and who, at the worst, if he fails, at least he fails while daring greatly so that his place shall never be with those cold and timid souls who knew neither victory nor defeat."
~Theodore Roosevelt, Citizenship in a Republic, 1910

HUDDLE TIME (10 MINS)
Question of the week: Besides your biblical mandate to serve, in what other areas do you serve God regularly?
"And One" Question
Pray for Each Other

NOTES:

"He begins to die, and that quits his desires." ~George Herbert

LEAD FROM THE BACK SERIES

TEAM MEETING 22
"SUPERVISE"

OPENING PRAYER (5 MINS)

HERO STORIES (5 MINS)

ROUND TABLE QUESTION (10 MINS)
What does lead from the back mean to you?

WEEKLY STUDY (30 MINS)
Read perhaps the three greatest scripture texts on God's guidance in situational decision-making:
Proverbs 3:5-6, Isaiah 30:21, and James 1:5

What is our role in the making of decisions based on what we think God is saying to us?

NOTES:

"Leadership is getting someone to do what they don't want to do, to achieve what they want to achieve." ~Tom Landry, Hall of Fame Football Coach

LEAD FROM THE BACK SERIES
TEAM MEETING 22 (CONT'D)

Remember Luke 22:24-27 from last week and the Disciples' argument over who was the greatest? Who do you think had the loudest voice in their dispute?

One might guess that Peter was in the middle of the "Who is the Greatest" argument. However, a few verses down in Luke 22:31-34, Jesus predicts Peter's failure. Why did Peter receive special coaching from Jesus?

In Luke 10:1-20 Jesus sends out The Seventy, including The Twelve. What can we determine about Jesus' supervisory leadership?
Matthew 28:16-20 and Luke 22:35

Coaches lead from the back. Military officers lead from the back. Leaders of larger organizations lead from the back. Rarely are they the tip of the spear. The only place a leader can see the big picture is in the back where he has greater visibility of the battles at hand.

NOTES:

LEAD FROM THE BACK SERIES
TEAM MEETING 22 (CONT'D)

What strategic reason would Jesus have for sending out The Seventy before the Great Commission?

Again, notice that Jesus employed the strategy of pairing up his men. Review why he did this in the Coaching Tips section.

> *"If I yell at you don't get upset, but if I ever stop then you had better worry because that'll be the day you're on the bench."*
> ~Jim Fazio, My High School Football Coach

Good leaders help followers get small wins under their belt. Why is it important we allow those we're coaching to experience success?

Jesus says, "Follow Me" 20 times. How can we resolve the tension between Jesus leading from the back and being the tip of the spear?
Matthew 4:19, 8:22, 9:9, 10:38, 16:24, and 19:21

NOTES:

LEAD FROM THE BACK SERIES
TEAM MEETING 22 (CONT'D)

Maybe this is the lost lesson of leadership for men that God has called to lead. Leading from the back is a call to sacrifice and service, but also to supervise. After a man has done everything to teach and train, letting others go ahead is an act of delegation and subsequent supervision. Maybe there is more than just humility going on here. Maybe it was a strategy of Jesus.

Why do you think Jesus, the coach, sent Peter to retrieve the coin out of the fish? Was this another supervisory test for his future leaders?
Matthew 17:25-27

This is the only time in the New Testament when a fish was caught with a hook (nets were normally used).

How can you implement Jesus' strategy to step back and supervise your family?

"The eye of the master will do more work than both of his hands."
~Benjamin Franklin

HUDDLE TIME (10 MINS)
Question of the week: Who do you need to coach and direct to a higher level?
"And One" Question
Pray for Each Other

NOTES:

"The secret to winning is constant, consistent management." ~Tom Landry

UNSWEPT CORNERS SERIES

TEAM MEETING 23
"SECRET LIES"

OPENING PRAYER (5 MINS)

HERO STORIES (5 MINS)

ROUND TABLE QUESTION (10 MINS)
How have you been impacted by someone else's secret?

WEEKLY STUDY (30 MINS)
Turn to 1 John 1:5-10. The subtitle in the English Standard Version of the Bible titles this section "Walking in the Light."

"If we claim to be without sin, we deceive ourselves and the truth is not in us. If we confess our sins, he is faithful and just and will forgive us our sins and purify us from all unrighteousness. If we claim we have not sinned, we make him out to be a liar and his word is not in us." ~Apostle John, 1 John 1:8-10

NOTES:

UNSWEPT CORNERS SERIES
TEAM MEETING 23 (CONT'D)

What does verse 5 teach us about God's nature?
Matthew 6:9, 1 Peter 1:14-16

The book of 1 John was written to refute Gnosticism. Gnosticism was a Greek philosophy that taught physical matter was evil and the spirit was good. It promoted a clear separation between the material and spiritual world. "Christian" Gnostics determined—since the matter was evil—God couldn't incarnate in a human body. He only appeared to be in human form and only appeared to suffer. It was an illusion. Two schools naturally appeared out of Gnosticism. One was extreme lust and gluttony, ignoring the body's health. The other practiced extreme discipline to punish the body into submission. The first Epistle of John was written to refute these views.

How does 1 John 1:6-7 contrast walking in darkness to walking in the light?
Matthew 6:22-23, John 1:5, 2 Corinthians 4:6, Ephesians 5:8, and Colossians 1:13-14

Jesus changes lives. To follow Jesus means to walk in the light. Explain verse 8 when it says, "The truth is not in us." Compare verse 8 to verse 10.

NOTES:

UNSWEPT CORNERS SERIES
TEAM MEETING 23 (CONT'D)

To walk in the light is to live a life of holiness. It's to become the best version of you with God's help.

Look at 1 John 1:9. We all struggle with sin. What does verse 9 promise about our struggle against sin?
Romans 3:10-12, 23, Job 42:6, and James 4:7-10

> *"He that is down needs fear no fall."* ~John Bunyan

The greatest sign of discipleship is a man's struggle to defeat sin.

Why is confession so tough? How is James 5:13-16 a game changer?

Get the lie out of your head that confession is for the weak. On the contrary, confession is only for the strong. Confession is manly.

NOTES:

UNSWEPT CORNERS SERIES
TEAM MEETING 23 (CONT'D)

How does a man mock God with his secret sins?
1 Corinthians 4:5 and Galatians 6:7-8

Secret sin is darkness. What do verses 7-8 guarantee to the man who mocks God?
1 Corinthians 6:9-10

Can you give some real-life examples (no names) of men who have done this?

HUDDLE TIME (10 MINS)
Question of the week: Are you walking in the dark right now? What sin is starting to scare you?
"And One" Question
Pray for Each Other

NOTES:

> "If a man cannot get through to God it is because there is a secret thing he does not intend to give up."
> ~Oswald Chambers

UNSWEPT CORNERS SERIES

TEAM MEETING 24
"WEAPONS OF MASS DESTRUCTION"

OPENING PRAYER (5 MINS)

HERO STORIES (5 MINS)

ROUND TABLE QUESTION (10 MINS)
What is the balance between appearing "judgy" (Matthew 7:1-5) and discerning a person's spiritual commitment based on the fruit of their lives (Matthew 7:13-20)?

WEEKLY STUDY (30 MINS)
"This is the message we have heard from him and declare to you: God is light; in him, there is no darkness at all. If we claim to have fellowship with him yet walk in the darkness, we lie and do not live by the truth. But if we walk in the light, as he is in the light, we have fellowship with one another, and the blood of Jesus, his Son, purifies us from all sin." ~Apostle John, 1 John 1:5-7

Compare the "darkness" mentioned in 1 John 1:5-7 and John 1:1-5. What discoveries can you see about darkness from John's perspective? Compare John's description of God having "no darkness at all" with Jesus' command to "be perfect." Matthew 5:48

NOTES:

"Lose the sex battle and defeat spreads into every portion of your being." ~E. Stanley Jones

UNSWEPT CORNERS SERIES
TEAM MEETING 24 (CONT'D)

How is a secret life of sin different than a blind spot?

What is the difference between darkness and "walking in darkness"? John 1:5 and 1 John 1:6

"Within each public person we see is another private person we can't see. The outer shell isn't the true person-only a covering behind which the true person lives. We dangerously assume the two correspond, but often they don't."
~Bill Perkins, 6 Battles Every Man Must Win

What is public evidence that a man is truly walking in the light?
Proverbs 27:17, John 13:34-35, and Hebrews 10:24-25

Fellowship with other believers is the first thing we pick up when we get serious about Jesus, and the first thing we put down when we start to drift.

How did Jesus deal with man's dark side of sin?
Matthew 6:12, James 5:16, 1 John 1:7, and 2:1

What do the following verses teach about living a secret life?
Proverbs 28:13 and 1 Corinthians 4:5

What warning does Solomon conclude? Ecclesiastes 12:13-14

What is even more frightening? Psalm 44:21, Romans 2:16, and Hebrews 4:13

HUDDLE TIME (10 MINS)
Question of the week: Where do you tend to dabble in darkness?
"And One" Question. Pray for Each Other.
NOTES:

"Sex is a wonderful servant but a terrible master." ~E Stanley Jones

UNSWEPT CORNERS SERIES

TEAM MEETING 25
"SECRET THREADS"

OPENING PRAYER (5 MINS)

HERO STORIES (5 MINS)

ROUND TABLE QUESTION (10 MINS)
What is an unswept corner?

WEEKLY STUDY (30 MINS)
"You shall not covet your neighbor's house. You shall not covet your neighbor's wife, or his manservant or maidservant, his ox or donkey, or anything that belongs to your neighbor." Exodus 20:17

What truth is there in the phrase, "You can't trust your best friend"?

NOTES:

*"I hate and regret the failure of my marriage.
I would gladly give all my millions for just one lasting marital success."*
~J. Paul Getty

UNSWEPT CORNERS SERIES
TEAM MEETING 25 (CONT'D)

Discuss the Marriage Saving Guardrails mentioned in the #1 bestseller *Strong Men Dangerous Times:*

1. Never develop an emotional connection with another woman.
2. Never be alone with a woman (closed doors, lunch meetings, car rides).
3. Never engage in any negative talk with a woman about your marriage, wife, or sex life.
4. Never compliment a woman in a way that would elicit an emotional response, unless your wife is somehow woven into the next sentence.
5. Never have a counseling relationship with another woman (one and done).
6. Never make physical contact with a sensual area (breasts, butt, face, leg, hand) of another woman.
7. Never make foul, rude, coarse, or sexual comments to a woman.
8. Never give a gift or card that is only from you (make it from you and your wife).
9. Never have non-business-related communication (text, DM, FB, calls).
10. Never assume your wife has the same guardrails. Be engaged!

Which one of these guardrails is currently your biggest issue?

NOTES:

"Don't ask yourself what the world needs. Ask yourself what makes you come alive, and then go do that. Because what the world needs is people who have come alive."
~Harold Thurman Whitman

UNSWEPT CORNERS SERIES
TEAM MEETING 25 (CONT'D)

From Deuteronomy 22:8. Why must a man build guardrails? Who will be hurt the most from your guardrail breach?

Guardrails were built around ancient rooftops to protect the homeowner's guests. In the same way, our moral guardrails protect not only us but the other people in our lives. And like the ancient guardrails, the guardrails you put in place can prevent severe harm or death!

What do the following verses tell us about the secret life of a man's eyes?
Proverbs 6:24-26, Matthew 5:28, and 1 John 2:16

After you draw a line that you'll never cross, proceed to stay as far away from it as possible.

What rule did Job have for his eyes? Do you have one? What is it?
Job 31:1

What is the wisdom against pornography from the following verses?
Proverbs 17:24 and Psalms 90:8 and 119:37

We are inundated with options for sexual sin like never before. A man can no longer be passive with this issue and walk in victory.

NOTES:

"There are two ways of spreading light: to be the candle or the mirror that reflects it."
~Edith Wharton

UNSWEPT CORNERS SERIES
TEAM MEETING 25 (CONT'D)

How do the Proverbs profile a dangerous woman?

- **She knows exactly what to say to attract a man.**
  Proverbs 2:16, 7:5, 7:21-23, 5:3, and 22:14

- **She acts according to society's accepted norm (she thinks she is right).**
  Proverbs 30:20

- **She has a way of making man forget the gravity of betrayal.**
  Proverbs 6:26, 7:14-15, and 24-27

HUDDLE TIME (10 MINS)
Question of the week: Is there any "other" woman in your life that others may see as a compromise of your Christian character and reputation? Do you have any secret or deleted threads with a woman who is not your wife and if found out, would damage your marriage?
"And One" Question
Pray for Each Other

NOTES:

"Don't judge what you don't know about me based only on what you know about yourself."
~Mike Yaconelli, Youth Specialties Founder

UNSWEPT CORNERS SERIES

TEAM MEETING 26
"SECRET LINKS"

OPENING PRAYER (5 MINS)

HERO STORIES (5 MINS)

ROUND TABLE QUESTION (10 MINS)
If your phone could talk, what would it say about you that others do not know?

WEEKLY STUDY (30 MINS)
Why is being "caught" in sin often the catalyst for change? What is the difference between repentance and the shame of being caught? Galatians 6:1

"Brothers, if anyone is caught in any transgression, you who are spiritual should restore him in a spirit of gentleness. Keep watch on yourself, lest you too be tempted. Bear one another's burdens, and so fulfill the law of Christ. For if anyone thinks he is something when he is nothing, he deceives himself. But let each one test his work, and then his reason to boast will be in himself alone and not in his neighbor. Each will have to bear his load." ~Apostle Paul, Galatians 6:1-5 (ESV)

What are some long-term signs of shame? Short-term?

NOTES:

"There is not enough darkness in all the world to put out the light of even one small candle." ~Robert Alden

UNSWEPT CORNERS SERIES
TEAM MEETING 26 (CONT'D)

What are some signs of true, biblical repentance? How are the fruits of the Spirit, deeds of repentance, and (life) by the Spirit similar? How are they different? Galatians 5:22-23, 6:1, and Acts 26:20

What is the danger when we judge others based on our sin of choice? Galatians 6:1-5

"A man cannot 'finish the course' or say that he's 'kept the faith' until he possesses a win-or-die attitude that resolves to 'fight the good fight' to his dying end." ~Anonymous

How does the process of carrying each other's burdens help to fight against judgment? Galatians 6:2, Matthew 7:1-5, Romans 3:10, and 23

How do you explain the apparent contradiction between Galatians 6:2 and 6:5?

Read John 8:1-11 out loud. How did Jesus—who never sinned (Hebrews 4:15)—deal with those who judged the woman's adultery? John 8:7-8

How did he treat the woman? John 8:11 and Galatians 6:3

If she was caught in the act of adultery, then where was the man (John 8:4)?

Why did Jesus judge men more harshly than the woman?

To the humble and broken, Jesus administered his mercy, but to the harsh and proud he delivered the Law.

What happens when guilt and shame wear off and a brother relapses? Matthew 18:15-20

HUDDLE TIME (10 MINS)
Question of the week: Share an area of your life where you are standing in judgment instead of carrying the load.
"And One" Question. Pray for Each Other.

"Discernment turns to judgment when you ask, 'Why?'"
~Chuck Swindoll

PROTECT THE BALL SERIES

TEAM MEETING 27
"JUST GET 'ER DONE"

OPENING PRAYER (5 MINS)

HERO STORIES (5 MINS)

ROUND TABLE QUESTION (10 MINS)
What are your thoughts on the statement, "What you do (for work) does not define who you are."

WEEKLY STUDY (30 MINS)
What is a biblical principle of work for the man of God?
2 Thessalonians 3:7-11 and Ephesians 4:28

Tentmaking involved handling urine. The great Apostle Paul made tents to help support his ministry. When his hands were not praying for others, they may have been softening leather with animal urine.

Discuss the balance between balancing work, marriage, and family.

What is the Christian response to the man who is capable of working but refuses?

"I like work: it fascinates me. I can sit and look at it for hours." ~Jerome K. Jerome

NOTES:

"Don't mistake activity for achievement." ~John Wooden

PROTECT THE BALL SERIES
TEAM MEETING 27 (CONT'D)

How should the man of God be a model in the workplace?
Colossians 3:22-23 and Ephesians 6:5-6

Discuss Charles Lamb's sarcastic remark, "I always arrive late at the office, but I make up for it by leaving early."

What is the balance between a man's priorities of work and leisure activities?
Proverbs 24:27 and 28:19

"When he worked, he worked. But when he played, he played." ~Dr. Seuss

What do these other proverbs say about work? Proverbs 12:11, 12:14, 14:23, 16:26, 21:25

"Without ambition one starts nothing. Without work one finishes nothing."
~Ralph Waldo Emerson

What should a man's role be in the local church? Matthew 9:37-38 and Ephesians 4:16

"I wish to preach, not on the doctrine of ignoble ease, but the doctrine of the strenuous life, the life of toil and effort, of labor and strife; to preach that higher form of success which comes, not to a man who desires mere easy peace, but to the man who does not shrink from danger, from hardship or bitter toil, and who out of these wins the splendid ultimate triumph." ~Theodore Roosevelt, 1899

HUDDLE TIME (10 MINS)
Question of the week: Would your boss/employees say your work ethic reflects your faith? Be honest.
"And One" Question. Pray for Each Other.

NOTES:

"Get going. Move forward. Aim High. Plan a takeoff. Don't just sit on the runway and hope someone will come along and push the airplane." ~Donald J. Trump, 45th President

PROTECT THE BALL SERIES

TEAM MEETING 28
"CUTS, SCARS, AND WOUNDS"

OPENING PRAYER (5 MINS)

HERO STORIES (5 MINS)

ROUND TABLE QUESTION (10 MINS)
Take 30 seconds to share one way your father wounded you. Where did he leave a scar?

"A wound that goes unacknowledged and unwept is a wound that cannot heal."
~John Eldredge

WEEKLY STUDY (30 MINS)
Discuss the ways the "quiver" mentioned in Psalm 127:4-5 protects the arrows and how that relates to fathering.

"Like arrows in the hands of a warrior are children born in one's youth. Blessed is the man whose quiver is full of them. They will not be put to shame when they contend with their opponents in court." ~Psalm 127:4-5 9 (NIV)

What are some practical ways a man can protect his children from harm's way? What can we learn from Job 1:4-5?

NOTES:

"I have been wounded but not yet slain. I shall lie here and bleed awhile. Then I shall rise and fight again. The title of champion may from time to time fall to others more than ourselves. But the heart, the spirit, and the soul of champions remain in Green Bay." ~Vince Lombardi

Men's Ministry Playbook - Page 122

PROTECT THE BALL
TEAM MEETING 28 (CONT'D)

"Your children are your reputation." ~Anonymous

What can you do as a father, husband, and man to ensure that your life and choices won't wound your children and godly heritage?
Exodus 20:4-6, 34:7, Deuteronomy 5:9, Numbers 14:18, and Jeremiah 32:18

What warning should a father heed about wounding his children?
Ephesians 6:4 and Colossians 3:21

"The spiritual life begins with the acceptance of our wounded self." ~Brennan Manning

How does exasperation lead to wounded adult children?

Exasperate. *Verb*: To cause great irritation or anger to; infuriate, to cause (an unpleasant feeling, condition, etc.), or to worsen; aggravate. *Adjective*: having a rough prickly surface because of the presence of hard projecting points. ~Collins English Dictionary

What is the tension between neglect and discipline in wounding our children?
Proverbs 3:1-2, 12, 13:24, 19:18-20, and Hebrews 12:8-9

What was Jesus' intent with Matthew 18:6? See verses 1-14

How might we encourage those we love when the wound is open and bleeding?
Jeremiah 31:13, Matthew 5:4, Romans 8:28, 12:15, and 2 Corinthians 12:9-10

"A wounded deer leaps the highest." ~Emily Dickinson

"Yes. True strength does not come out of bravado. Until we are broken, our life will be self-centered, self-reliant; our strength will be our own." ~John Eldredge, *Wild at Heart*

HUDDLE TIME (10 MINS)
Question of the week: What are some guardrails you can build around your children now to protect them from wounds down the road?
"And One" Question. Pray for Each Other.

"A child rightly trained may be a worldwide blessing, with an influence reaching onward to eternal years. But a neglected or misdirected child may live to blight and blast mankind and leave influences of evil which shall roll on in increasing volume till they plunge into the gulf of eternal perdition." ~George Muller

PROTECT THE BALL SERIES
TEAM MEETING 29
"YOUR BODY"

OPENING PRAYER (5 MINS)

HERO STORIES (5 MINS)

ROUND TABLE QUESTION (10 MINS)
What are you learning about your body as you age?

WEEKLY STUDY (30 MINS)
Why should we steward our bodies well? Proverbs 3:7-8 and 1 Corinthians 6:19-20

"Take care of your body. It's the only place you have to live." ~Jim Rohn

How are our bodies unique from women? What does that say about why God made us that way who follow Jesus? John 14:17, 20:22, Acts 1:8, and Romans 5:5, 8:11

"The body too, has its rights, and it will have them: they cannot be trampled on without peril. The body ought to be the soul's best friend. Many good men however have neglected to make it such: so it has become a fiend and has plagued them." ~Augustus and Charles Hare, 1827

What is a healthy perspective about our bodies?
2 Corinthians 4:16-18 and 1 Timothy 4:8

NOTES:

"The body never lies."
~Martha Graham

"Scars are tattoos with better stories."
~Toyota Ad, *Sports Illustrated*, June 2002

PROTECT THE BALL SERIES
TEAM MEETING 29 (CONT'D)

"Man is an intelligence in servitude to his organs." ~Aldous Huxley

What great rule of thumb does the Bible offer regarding what we allow into our bodies? 1 Corinthians 6:12, 10:31, and 2 Peter 2:19

"Some people have a foolish way of not minding, or pretending not to mind, what they eat. For my part, I mind my belly very studiously, and very carefully; for I look upon it, that he who does not mind his belly will hardly mind anything else." ~Samuel Johnson

How does the fruit of self-control affect the whole man?
Proverbs 16:32, 25:28 and Galatians 5:22-23

"Tis in ourselves that we are thus or thus. Our bodies are our gardens to which our wills are gardeners." ~William Shakespeare, Othello

What are your thoughts about the value of spiritual leadership and the fruit of self-control from the pastoral epistles? 1 Timothy 3:2, 2 Timothy 3:3, Titus 1:8, 2:2, 2:6, and 2:12

The three Pastoral Epistles are books of the New Testament: 1 Timothy, 2 Timothy, and the Epistle to Titus. They are letters from Paul Timothy and Titus. They are generally discussed as a group (sometimes with the addition of the Epistle to Philemon) and are given the title 'Pastoral' because they are addressed to individuals with pastoral oversight of churches and discuss issues of Christian living, doctrine, and leadership.

"The pain of being overweight is far worse than the pain of working out." ~FitnessMotivated.com

HUDDLE TIME (10 MINS)
My body is telling me to...
"And One" Question. Pray for Each Other.

"We are very concerned with the level of childhood obesity... We don't want this generation of young people to live fewer years than their parents." ~Mike Johanns U.S. Senator

PROTECT THE BALL SERIES

TEAM MEETING 30
"FRIENDLY FIRE"

OPENING PRAYER (5 MINS)

HERO STORIES (5 MINS)

ROUND TABLE QUESTION (10 MINS)
Share the name of one man who has your permission to call you in, call you up and call you out, and regularly does it.

WEEKLY STUDY (30 MINS)

"True friends dare to call each other out." ~ Anonymous

In the Round Table Question we asked about who has your permission to call you in, call you up, and call you out. What does each of these mean?

My best friend calls me into places I would never venture alone, calls out the best in me, and calls me up to a higher plain of life.

Discuss the meaning of Proverbs 27:5-6. Luke 17:3-4 and Proverbs 28:23

Sometimes getting called out needs to come sooner rather than later.

What is the proper way to handle someone who has rightfully called you out? Proverbs 25:12?

NOTES:

"All daring and courage, all iron endurance of misfortune make for a finer and nobler type of manhood." ~Theodore Roosevelt, 1897

PROTECT THE BALL SERIES
TEAM MEETING 30 (CONT'D)

What is the goal when rebuking another? Proverbs 1:22-23, 3:11-12, 13:1, 17:10, 19:25

What process should be employed when rebuking someone?
Proverbs 9:8, Matthew 18:15-18, and Galatians 6:1-2

"Better is open rebuke than hidden love. Wounds from a friend can be trusted, but an enemy multiplies kisses." ~Proverbs 27:5-6

What are some guidelines when rebuking a brother? Ephesians 4:15 and 29

If we say we have someone's back, maybe we should protect them when we see the knife coming.

"It may be the part of a friend to rebuke a friend's folly." ~J.R.R. Tolkien

What does "Faithful are the wounds of a friend" (NASB) in Proverbs 27:6 mean as it relates to friendship?

What does verse 6 mean when it says, "But [deceitful are the kisses of an enemy?" Matthew 26:48-49

The kiss is common in eastern lands in salutation, on the cheek, the forehead, the beard, the hands, and the feet, but not (in Palestine) the lips.

"A winner rebukes and forgives; a loser is too timid to rebuke and too petty to forgive."
~Sydney J. Harris

HUDDLE TIME (10 MINS)
Question of the week: Where can you be a better friend in calling a buddy out on his blind spot?
"And One" Question.
Pray for Each Other

"Next to a sincere compliment, I think I like a well-deserved and honest rebuke." ~William Feather

IRON MEN SERIES

TEAM MEETING 31
"SMELL OF IRON"

OPENING PRAYER (5 MINS)

HERO STORIES (5 MINS)

ROUND TABLE QUESTION (10 MINS)
What does it mean to have a friend that is closer to you than a brother?

WEEKLY STUDY (30 MINS)
Can you think of a certain smell that elicits a fond memory? Some of the smells that take me back to my younger, glory, days are the fresh-cut grass on a football field, the smell of a cold basketball court, the musk of the locker room, and the smell of iron in the weight. I can't explain it, but it was there nonetheless.

Choose someone to read Proverbs 27:9-10.

"Oil and perfume make the heart glad, so a man's counsel is sweet to his friend. Do not forsake your own friend or your father's friend, and do not go to your brother's house in the day of your calamity; better is a neighbor who is near than a brother far away." ~Proverbs 27:9-10 (NASB)

NOTES:

IRON MEN SERIES
TEAM MEETING 31 (CONT'D)

How are perfume and incense compared to the "counsel" of a friend?

What different Bible translations of verse 9 do you have? Which do you prefer?

"The sweetness of his friend from the counsel of soul."
~Hebrew translation

"The soul is sweetened by the good counsels of a friend."
~Latin translation

"The counsel of a friend is sweeter than one's advice."
~G.R. Driver translation

"A friend who is available is better than a relative who is not."
~Expositor's Bible Commentary

How should a friend watch your back?
Job 16:20-21, Ecclesiastes 4:10, 1 Samuel 22:23, and Proverbs 17:17

NOTES:

IRON MEN SERIES
TEAM MEETING 31 (CONT'D)

"Who's got my back now? When all we have left is deceptive, so disconnected. So what is the truth now? There's still time, all that has been devastated can be recreated. Realize, we pick up the broken pieces of our lives giving ourselves to each other, ourselves to each other—to rest our head on."
~The Band Creed, Who's Got My Back?

Discuss verse 10, "Do not forsake your own friend or your father's friend, and do not go to your brother's house in the day of your calamity; better is a neighbor who is near than a brother far away?"

"The worst solitude is to have no real friendships." ~Francis Bacon

Compare Proverbs 27:10 with Proverbs 18:24.

"Keeping score is for games, not friendships." ~John C. Maxwell

What are your thoughts about the above quote?

NOTES:

IRON MEN SERIES
TEAM MEETING 31 (CONT'D)

Which statement holds more truth: Verse 10 (above) or the saying "blood is thicker than water"? Why?

"Friendships are discovered rather than made." ~Harriet Beecher Stowe

Finish the sentence: I'm the kind of friend that...

"Friendships born on the field of athletic strife are the real gold of competition. Awards become corroded; friends gather no dust." ~Jesse Owens

HUDDLE TIME (10 MINS)
Question of the week: Who's got your back?
"And One" Question
Pray for Each Other

NOTES:

Keep your friends close and your enemies closer.
~Secular Proverb

IRON MEN SERIES

TEAM MEETING 32
"SHARPEN YOUR FACE"

OPENING PRAYER (5 MINS)

HERO STORIES (5 MINS)

ROUND TABLE QUESTION (10 MINS)
When I think of iron sharpening iron, I think of...

WEEKLY STUDY (30 MINS)
In blade sharpening, there is always the edge being sharpened and the stronger substance, usually dull and stronger, is the sharpening agent. There is one or the other, but not at the same time. Healthy relationships work similarly. At times, one sharpens a friend who needs it, and sometimes it changes. To be healthy (non-co-dependent) relationships, there must be a sharpening exchange, so-to-speak.

What is more important, the appearance of a man's face or his countenance?

NOTES:

IRON MEN SERIES
TEAM MEETING 32 (CONT'D)

"Iron sharpeneth iron; so a man sharpeneth the countenance of his friend."
~Proverbs 27:17 (KJV)

"The word for "countenance" used in the King James Version above is the Hebrew word pene. Pene is the Hebrew word for face. The word pene (face) must mean here the personality or character of the individual." ~Expositors Bible Commentary

Here are some different translations of the same verse. Which one resonates with you?

"As iron sharpens iron, so a man sharpens the countenance of his friend."
~New King James Version

"As iron sharpens iron, so a friend sharpens a friend."
~New Living Translation

"As iron sharpens iron, so one man sharpens another."
~New American Standard Version

"As iron sharpens iron, so one person sharpens another."
~New International Version

"Iron sharpens iron, and one man sharpens another."
~English Standard Version

"You use steel to sharpen steel, and one friend sharpens another."
~The Message (Paraphrase)

How would you translate Proverbs 27:17 based on what you now know about the Hebrew word *pene* or face?

IRON MEN SERIES
TEAM MEETING 32 (CONT'D)

"One man in a thousand, Solomon says, will stick closer than a brother. And it's worthwhile seeking him half your days if you find him before the other. Nine-hundred and ninety-nine depend on what the world sees in you, but the Thousandth Man will stand your friend with the whole round world against you."
~Rudyard Kipling, The Thousandth Man (poem) NOTES

"Fathers are to sons what blacksmiths are to swords. It is the job of the blacksmith not only to make the sword but also to maintain its edge of sharpness. It is the job of the father to keep his son sharp and save him from the dullness of foolishness. He gives his son that sharp edge through discipline." ~Steve Farrar

The two other times pene is used in the bible are Numbers 6:22-27 (verses 25 and 26). How do your various Bible translations interpret *pene* here?

NOTES:

IRON MEN SERIES
TEAM MEETING 32 (CONT'D)

"As hard iron or steel, will bring a knife to a better edge when it is properly whetted against it: so one friend may be the means of exciting another to reflect, (or) dive deeply into, an illustrate subject, without which whetting or excitement, this had never taken place." ~Adam Clarke Commentary

What does a sharp face look like? How does it live?

Tie Ecclesiastes 10:10 and Proverbs 27:17 together.

Share a story about a time another man sharpened your face.

"But let me sharpen others as the hone gives the edge to razors, though itself has none."
~St. Francis of Assisi

Now compare Proverbs 27:17 with Hebrews 4:12.

What men have you invited to sharpen you and judge the "thoughts and intentions of your heart?"

HUDDLE TIME (10 MINS)
Question of the week: What needs to be sharpened in your life and who might be able to help?
"And One" Question
Pray for Each Other

NOTES:

"Two minds acting on each other become more acute."
~Barnes Notes

IRON MEN SERIES

TEAM MEETING 33
"REFLECTIONS"

OPENING PRAYER (5 MINS)

HERO STORIES (5 MINS)

ROUND TABLE QUESTION (10 MINS)
When do you take time to think or reflect?

WEEKLY STUDY (30 MINS)
What are some ways to see glimpses into a man's heart?

"As in water face reflects face so the heart of man reflects man." ~Proverbs 27:19

"There are several suggestions as to the meaning of this proverb. First, the simplest way to take the verse is to say that, "as clear water gives a reflection of the face, so the heart reflects the true nature of the man" (NIV). Second, another suggestion is, "through the observation of another, man can know himself". The point seems to be that it is through looking at our heart attitudes that we come to true self-awareness." ~Expositor's Bible Commentary

In face-sharpening relationships, how do you balance helpful discernment with judgment? Matthew 7:1-5 and 15-20

NOTES:

IRON MEN SERIES
TEAM MEETING 33 (CONT'D)

What is the difference between judging the fruit of one's life and judging the person?

What are your thoughts about Adam Clarke's alternate translation of Proverbs 27:19 (below)?

"Or, as a man sees his face perfectly reflected by the water when looking into it; so the wise and penetrating man sees generally what is in the heart of another by considering the general tenor of his words and actions."
~Adam Clarke's Commentary

Esse quam videri. Translation: To be, rather than to appear.

What are some ways to discern what's on the inside based on what we hear outside? Matthew 12:33-37 and 15:18-20

What's one problem when we assume what we see and hear is a heart issue? Jeremiah 17:9 and 1 Corinthians 2:11

What must we understand when sharpening a friend? Psalm 139:1-4 and Jeremiah 12:3a

How is your heart for God being reflected in those you love?

HUDDLE TIME (10 MINS)
Question of the week: Where can you improve in reflecting on your relationship with God with your inner circle?
"And One" Question
Pray for Each Other

"Life needs a man to be fierce—and fiercely devoted."
~John Eldredge

THE WILD SIDE SERIES

TEAM MEETING 34
"LIVING DANGEROUSLY"

OPENING PRAYER (5 MINS)

HERO STORIES (5 MINS)

ROUND TABLE QUESTION (10 MINS)
If you were given twenty-five thousand dollars, and one week to spend it with the three stipulations: 1) you had to do it with a friend, 2) you had to spend all the money, and 3) it had to be something that fueled your fire. What would it be?

WEEKLY STUDY (30 MINS)
What are some dangers of living dangerously?

Compare the creation of Adam in Genesis 2:4-9 to the creation of Eve in verses Genesis 2:18-25. Where were they created and what might that say about each?

NOTES:

"Instead of praying 'If I die before a wake' we should pray 'If I wake before I die.' "
~Dr. Anthony Campolo

THE WILD SIDE SERIES
TEAM MEETING 34 (CONT'D)

"Eve was created within the lush beauty of Eden's Garden. But Adam if you'll remember, was created outside the garden, in the wilderness. A man was born in the outback, from the untamed part of creation. Only afterward is he brought into Eden. And ever since then boys have never been at home indoors, and men have had an insatiable desire to explore. We long to return; it's when most men come alive."
~John Eldredge, Wild at Heart

Is the desire for the wild side, the adventurous life, from God, or is it something men fabricate? What role does adventure play when men live the "full life"?
John 10:10b

"He was mastered by the sheer surging of life, the tidal wave of being, the perfect joy of each separate muscle, joint, and sinew in that it was everything that was not death, that it was aglow and rampant, expressing itself in movement, flying exultingly under the stars. " ~Jack London, *The Call of the Wild*

The Greek word for life is *zoe*. *Zoe* speaks of the life that is given by God through Christ Jesus to those who believe the gospel. It means life "eternal," "everlasting," or "of endless duration." In other words, it refers to a life that starts the moment a man receives Jesus and continues through eternity. It's eternal life starting now!

What threatens to rob men of their passion to live a full life of adventure?

"Every man dies. Not every man truly lives."
~William Wallace, The Movie, Braveheart

"Adventure, with its requisite danger and wildness, is a deeply spiritual longing written into the soul of man...Every man has an adventure to live."
~John Eldredge, *Wild at Heart*

What's the balance between accepting responsibility for those we are called to lead and living adventurously?

Where do you draw the line between fun and foolishness?

THE WILD SIDE SERIES
TEAM MEETING 34 (CONT'D)

"When a man comes to the mountains he comes home."
~John Muir

Single men, what are your thoughts about adventure? Men with kids in and out of the home, what lessons would you like to share with the younger men? Grandpas and elder statesmen, share your wisdom with us all.

"Men need to bark at the moon. Men need to blow something up. Men need to push themselves into a zone they don't control—that isn't a zone. Men need to go in pursuit. They need a quest."
~Steven Mansfield, Mansfield's Book of Manly Men

Let's look at the temptation of Jesus. Before he was released into public ministry, the Spirit led him into the wilderness. Why?
Matthew 4:1 and Luke 4:1.

"The only difference between a rut and the grave is the size of the hole."
~Unknown

Read the account of Jacob. Where do you go to wrestle with God?
Genesis 32:9-12 and 22-26.

"How we need men who refuse to let biology define their destiny and who live inspired by a fiery inner vision of the masculine life."
~Steven Mansfield

NOTES:

THE WILD SIDE SERIES
TEAM MEETING 34 (CONT'D)

What does Matthew 11:11-15 (specifically verse 12) stir up in you?

"A manly man is not without fear; rather he overcomes his fear by enduring difficulty and hardship."
~General William G. Boykin

Where do you need God to disturb the monotony of your life? Where do you need God to fire you up? Where do you need to rekindle your passion for adventure?

"Disturb us, Lord, to dare more boldly, to venture on wider seas where storms will show your mastery; where losing sight of land we shall find the stars."
~Sir Francis Drake

"The great danger for most of us is not that our aim is too high and we miss it, but that it is too low and we reach it."
~Michelangelo

HUDDLE TIME (10 MINS)
Question of the week: Where do you need to rediscover your adventurous self?
"And One" Question
Pray for Each Other

NOTES:

"Only those who risk going too far can find out how far one can go."
~T.S. Elliot

THE WILD SIDE SERIES
TEAM MEETING 35
"A GOOD MAN'S GUILT"

OPENING PRAYER (5 MINS)

HERO STORIES (5 MINS)

ROUND TABLE QUESTION (10 MINS)
How does the guilt that good and godly men experience when enjoying life hinder them from living to the fullest?

WEEKLY STUDY (30 MINS)
This meeting was inspired by the good and godly men in my life who are dominated by a form of guilt that is not from God. This team meeting is designed to free good, hard-working, Kingdom-minded men from guilt, and permit them to have fun, enjoy life, and renew their strength while enjoying life-giving experiences.

Why do good men experience guilt when they take time to enjoy life?

NOTES:

"You'll pay a very high price for doing nothing for your boy."
~William Beausay II

THE WILD SIDE SERIES
TEAM MEETING 35 (CONT'D)

Guilt is only justified when we disobey the Word of God and are guilty of unrepented sin.
Matthew 26:74-75 and 27:4-6

How do we know when we have crossed over from enjoying life to abusing it?

STORY: There's an old legend that the Apostle John used to care for pigeons as a hobby.

One day, as he was caring for his birds, a man, bow in hand, walked by after a long day of hunting and joked, "Ha, the great apostle is tending to the pigeons!"

John looked at the man and asked, "I noticed you have your bow unstrung. Why is that?"

The man replied, "I remove the string from my bow after hunting so the constant pressure will not cause the bow to break or fracture due to constant stress."

"That, my friend," smiled John, "is why I tend to the pigeons."

What's the purpose of enjoying our hobbies?

NOTES:

THE WILD SIDE SERIES
TEAM MEETING 35 (CONT'D)

"Good and godly men often accuse themselves of sins they do not commit and experience guilt that is not from God, which leads to a different kind of Bondage—martyrdom."
~Anonymous

Do you think Peter was going to work or to relax?
John 21:1-3

"Will you choose to build a monument to your compromises, rather than a bold and fruitful life? What kind of man will you be? What will you instill in your children—courage or fear?"
~Ed McGlasson

How does the Holy Spirit help us find the balance between living on the responsible wild side and the wild, irresponsible, side of life?
Isaiah 30:21, Proverbs 3:5-6, John 3:8, 14:15-18, 26, and 16:12-15

What is the difference between feeling guilty and being guilty?
Ephesians 2:8-10, 1 Peter 2:24 and 3:18

NOTES:

THE WILD SIDE SERIES
TEAM MEETING 35 (CONT'D)

"The work must be done; we cannot escape our responsibility; and if we are worth our salt, we shall be glad of the chance to do the work."
~Theodore Roosevelt

How does Romans 8:1 encourage those men who wrongfully walk in guilt?

Is it selfish for a good man to take the time to enjoy the pleasures of life even if that means getting away from his family?

How can we use other men to help us determine the right balance between enjoying life and selfishness?
1 John 1:9 and James 5:13-16

HUDDLE TIME (10 MINS)
Question of the week: How can we pray over the unjustifiable guilt you may be experiencing?
"And One" Question
Pray for Each Other

NOTES:

"Holiness is allowing God to fill every corner of your being; that is when we truly become the best version- of ourselves." ~Matthew Kelly

THE WILD SIDE SERIES
TEAM MEETING 36
"FIGHTING SIN"

OPENING PRAYER (5 MINS)

HERO STORIES (5 MINS)

ROUND TABLE QUESTION (10 MINS)
Share one battle that may be preventing you from living out the wild side of the life God has intended for you.

WEEKLY STUDY (30 MINS)
In his book *Wild at Heart*, John Eldredge states that, among other things, every man has a "battle to fight." What does this mean?

Where can you find men in Scripture fighting personal battles?

NOTES:

"Masculinity is not something given to you, but something you gain. And you gain it by winning small battles with honor."
~Norman Mailer

THE WILD SIDE SERIES
TEAM MEETING 36 (CONT'D)

Did you in the past have a struggle like that from which you eventually emerged in victory?

Are you involved right now in a struggle like that?

> *"Great men suffer greatly to be great. Heroic men must first endure heroic struggles with themselves."*
> ~Steven Mansfield, *The Conflict of Two Natures*

What are some truths about sin?
Romans 3:9-10, 3:21-24, 5:6-8, 6:20-23, and Hebrews 4:15

How are we to understand the next words from Romans 7:25, "Thanks be to God—through Jesus Christ our Lord!"

NOTES:

THE WILD SIDE SERIES
TEAM MEETING 36 (CONT'D)

"For we know that the Law is spiritual, but I am of flesh, sold into bondage to sin. For what I am doing, I do not understand; for I am not practicing what I would like to do, but I am doing the very thing I hate. But if I do the very thing I do not want to do, I agree with the Law, confessing that the Law is good. So now, no longer am I the one doing it, but sin which dwells in me. For I know that nothing good dwells in me, that is, in my flesh; for the willing is present in me, but the doing of the good is not. For the good that I want, I do not do, but I practice the very evil that I do not want. But if I am doing the very thing I do not want, I am no longer the one doing it, but sin which dwells in me. I find then the principle that evil is present in me, the one who wants to do good. For I joyfully concur with the law of God in the inner man, but I see a different law in the members of my body, waging war against the law of my mind and making me a prisoner of the law of sin which is in my members. Wretched man that I am! Who will set me free from the body of this death?"

~Romans 7:14-24 (NIV)

NOTES:

THE WILD SIDE SERIES
TEAM MEETING 36 (CONT'D)

"The things we celebrated before Christ we're ashamed of now.
Shame leads to secrets. Secrets can lead to bondage."
~Jim Ramos

How are sin and temptation different?
Matthew 4:1-11 and James 1:13-15

What do we know about temptation?
1 Corinthians 10:13

Where do you need to battle fiercely against the sin that hinders your relationship with God?

"In every relationship, something fierce is needed once in a while."
~Robert Bly

HUDDLE TIME (10 MINS)
Question of the week: What is the dominant temptation in your life?
"And One" Question
Pray for Each Other

NOTES:

"We gain strength from the temptations we resist." ~Ralph Waldo Emerson

IN MEN, WE TRUST SERIES

TEAM MEETING 37
"FIGHT FOR HER"

OPENING PRAYER (5 MINS)

HERO STORIES (5 MINS)

ROUND TABLE QUESTION (10 MINS)
What does it mean to fight for your wife?

WEEKLY STUDY (30 MINS)
This study is based on thoughts I took from my bride, Shanna when I asked her where men need to fight for their marriages. I'm not sure if that meant they are areas I need to work on, do well in, or men generally need to know! This is a different study than we normally have. And I hope you enjoy the change.

In what areas do you fight for your wife regularly?

NOTES:

"Often fighting for your wife means fighting with your wife." ~Jim Ramos

IN MEN, WE TRUST SERIES
TEAM MEETING 37 (CONT'D)

When a woman trusts she is loved and accepted for who she is, when she trusts she is first on her husband's list, and when she knows there is no competition, most of the struggle of living together dissipates.

Consider how Jesus fought for us and discuss how we can imitate Jesus by fighting for our brides.
Ephesians 5:25-33

Verse 25: "He gave himself up for us."
1 Corinthians 15:3-4 and 1 Peter 3:18

Verse 26: "He cleansed us."
Ephesians 1:7 and 1 John 1:9

Verse 27: He "present(s)" us to God.
John 14:6 and 1 Timothy 2:3-6

"A happy marriage is the union of two good forgivers."
~Robert Quillen

NOTES:

IN MEN, WE TRUST SERIES
TEAM MEETING 37 (CONT'D)

Verse 29: He "feed(s) and care(s)" for us.
Philippians 4:19 and 1 Peter 5:6-7

> *"Don't marry the person you think you can live with; marry only the individual you think you can't live without."*
> ~James C. Dobson

Verses 31-32: He is "united" to us.
John 14:17 and 1 Corinthians 6:19-20

> *"A man wants to be a hero to the beauty. It's not enough to be a hero; it's to be a hero to the woman he loves. Not every woman wants a battle to fight, but every woman yearns to be fought for. She wants more than to be noticed—she wants to be wanted."*
> ~John Eldredge, *Wild at Heart*

NOTES:

IN MEN, WE TRUST SERIES
TEAM MEETING 37 (CONT'D)

Discuss "Shanna's Fight List" for men. Shanna is the wife of Men in the Arena Founder, Jim Ramos.

1. Fight to honor her publicly

"There is something fierce in every man. A man needs a battle to fight; he needs a place for the warrior in him to come alive and be honed, trained, and seasoned."
~John Eldredge, *Wild at Heart*

2. Fight to protect her

3. Fight for the integrity of the family unit

"Coming together is a beginning; keeping together is progress; working together is a success." ~Henry Ford

4. Fight to earn her respect

"We come to love not by finding a perfect person, but by learning to see an imperfect person perfectly." ~Sam Keen

5. Fight to make her feel safe and secure

6. Fight to lead her spiritually

"The older I get, the less time I want to spend with the part of the human race that didn't marry me." ~Robert Brault

HUDDLE TIME (10 MINS)
Question of the week: Which of "Shanna's Fight List" items do you need to work on the most?
"And One" Question. Pray for Each Other.

"Fine speech. Now what do we do? Just be yourselves. Where are you going? I'm going to pick a fight."
~William Wallace to Stephen, The Movie, Braveheart

Men's Ministry Playbook - Page 153

IN MEN, WE TRUST SERIES

TEAM MEETING 38
"GOD>WIFE>KIDS"

OPENING PRAYER (5 MINS)

HERO STORIES (5 MINS)

ROUND TABLE QUESTION (10 MINS)
What do you (or will you) do regularly to affirm that your wife is the most important person in your life?

WEEKLY STUDY (30 MINS)
The order in which things appear was critically important to the ancient Jews. We see this in the list of The Twelve and the Household Codes. What priority has God given to husbands?
Ephesians 5:25-33, Colossians 3;18-22, and 1 Peter 3:1-7

We must get over the lie that our children are more important than our wives. If our children are truly important then loving their mom will be an even higher priority than loving them.

Should the kids take priority over the wife in second or third marriages?
NOTES:

"The best thing a father can do for his children is to love their mother."
~John Wooden, Legendary Basketball Coach

IN MEN, WE TRUST SERIES
TEAM MEETING 38 (CONT'D)

Did you know that Bathsheba is always referred to as "the Wife of Uriah the Hittite" even after she married King David? In the Bible, God only recognizes the first marriage unless there is a death of a spouse.

What does Ephesians 5:25 mean when it admonishes husbands to, "Love your wives, just as Christ loved the church and gave himself up for her"?
Colossians 3:19 and 1 Peter 3:7

"She trusts you when you keep your covenant with God and one another as your top priority. Trust is based on a relentless commitment to your covenant with God and one another. Ultimately a man's behavior speaks the loudest to a woman. While words are important, trust will not occur until the words are backed with action."
~Anonymous Wife

What are some things you can do to love your wife as Christ loved the church?

"You don't marry one person; you marry three: the person you think they are, the person they are, and the person they are going to become as a result of being married to you."
~Richard Needham

NOTES:

IN MEN, WE TRUST SERIES
TEAM MEETING 38 (CONT'D)

What does it look like when we make our wives holy?
Ephesians 5:26-27

"Hágios (holy) has the technical meaning of being different from the world. Hágios (God's word for holy) implies something set apart and therefore different, distinguished, or distinct."
~Strong's Bible Concordance

What are some creative ways for husbands to wash their wives "through the word"?

"My most brilliant achievement was my ability to be able to persuade my wife to marry me." ~ Winston Churchill

How can we make our wives such a priority that they are "without stain or wrinkle or any other blemish, but holy and blameless"?
Ephesians 5:27

"There is no greater happiness for a man than approaching a door at the end of the day knowing someone on the other side of that door is waiting for the sound of his footsteps."
~Ronald Reagan

What can be some problems with the loving-our-wives-like-our-bodies illustration? What are some benefits?
Ephesians 5:28 and 33

NOTES:

IN MEN, WE TRUST SERIES
TEAM MEETING 38 (CONT'D)

How do we tie it all together?
Ephesians 5:31-31, Genesis 2:24 and Matthew 19:5-6

"Marriage has the power to set the course of your life as a whole. If your marriage is strong, even if all the circumstances in your life around you are filled with trouble and weakness, it won't matter. You will be able to move out into the world in strength." ~Timothy Keller

"To find someone who will love you for no reason, and to shower that person with reasons, is the ultimate happiness." ~Robert Brault

Tools for the marriage toolbox.
1. Weekly Date Night
2. Daily Act of Service
3. Something Spiritual Daily
4. What other ideas can you come up with to make your wife a priority?

HUDDLE TIME (10 MINS)
Question of the week: What one thing can you do to show your wife she is the number one person in your life?
"And One" Question
Pray for Each Other

NOTES:

"I have learned that only two things are necessary to keep one's wife happy. First, let her think she's having her way. And second, let her have it."
~Lyndon B. Johnson

IN MEN, WE TRUST SERIES
TEAM MEETING 39
"TARGET HER TRUST"

OPENING PRAYER (5 MINS)

HERO STORIES (5 MINS)

ROUND TABLE QUESTION (10 MINS)
What does it mean to target your wife's trust?

WEEKLY STUDY (30 MINS)
To target our wife's trust (future wife for single men) is first and foremost to be a man worthy of trust. Let's have each man share and explain one characteristic of being trustworthy.

What does the Bible teach about the character and nature of God and His Word?
Psalm 19:7, 111:7-8, 119:86 and 119:138

Definitions of Trustworthy:
"Able to be relied on to do or provide what is needed or right: deserving of trust."
~Merriam-Webster Dictionary
"Able to be relied on as honest or truthful." ~Oxford Dictionary

NOTES:

IN MEN, WE TRUST SERIES
TEAM MEETING 39 (CONT'D)

"I've trusted you for twenty years and you've never let me down. I'll trust you (without any source of income) to leave the church and launch Men in the Arena."
~Shanna Ramos, 2012 Family Breakfast

What do the following Proverbs teach about the qualities of a man worthy of trust? Proverbs 11:13, 12:22, 13:17 and 25:13

"Men in the Arena transformed my husband into the man I always knew he could be." ~Kelly

What is the value of faithfulness in leadership? 2 Timothy 2:2

"Because of what God did in my husband through Men in the Arena, my daughters finally have a man to measure all men against." ~Riane

What wisdom can we learn about building? 1 Corinthians 13:1-8

Trustworthy implies being worthy of, or earning trust. Is trust in a marriage earned or given? Explain. Exodus 18:20-22, Nehemiah 13:12-13

"Whether things are sailing smoothly or the bottom has dropped out, He is always trustworthy. You can count on Almighty God to keep His everlasting Word."
~Charles Stanley

"Manhood is protecting integrity, fighting apathy, pursuing God passionately, leading courageously, and finishing strong." ~Jim Ramos, *Strong Men Dangerous Times*

HUDDLE TIME (10 MINS)
Question of the week: What area do you need to target trust in your marriage?
"And One" Question. Pray for Each Other.

"The chief lesson I have learned in a long life is that the only way you can make a man trustworthy is to trust him, and the surest way to make him untrustworthy is to distrust him."
~Henry L. Stimson

IN MEN, WE TRUST SERIES

TEAM MEETING 40
"SECURITY GLAND"

OPENING PRAYER (5 MINS)

HERO STORIES (5 MINS)

ROUND TABLE QUESTION (10 MINS)
When we speak of man "providing" for his wife, what does that mean?

WEEKLY STUDY (30 MINS)
Today we are going to break into our Huddles (two pairs of two) for our study. Read Kelly's, wife of an Arena Man, quote. What do you think she meant by "everything?"

> "Women trust their husbands when he does everything they can to provide for their family." ~Kelly

Use a concordance on your Bible app or the back of your Bible to find support verses for each of the items on your "everything" list.

NOTES:

IN MEN, WE TRUST SERIES
TEAM MEETING 40 (CONT'D)

Earning a living is only one aspect of providing, but it is not the most important. What things should take priority over earning a living? How would a Christian man living in poverty respond?

> *"Women are created with a small gland that men don't have. It's called the security gland."*
> ~Dave Ramsey

Come back together as a team. Choose the man who has been married the longest to be the spokesman and share your results, along with support verses, to the rest of the team.

> *"Try not to become a man of success, but rather try to become a man of value."*
> ~Albert Einstein

> *"Security is mostly a superstition. It does not exist in nature, nor do the children of men as a whole experience it. Avoiding danger is no safer in the long run than outright exposure. Life is either a daring adventure or nothing."*
> ~Helen Keller

HUDDLE TIME (10 MINS)
Question of the week: Where can you grow as a provider?
"And One" Question
Pray for Each Other

NOTES:

> *"Nothing can bring a real sense of security into the home except true love."* ~Billy Graham

IN MEN, WE TRUST SERIES

TEAM MEETING 41
"MARRIAGE COVENANT VS. CONTRACT"

OPENING PRAYER (5 MINS)

HERO STORIES (5 MINS)

ROUND TABLE QUESTION (10 MINS)
When was the last time you read your marriage vows and what stood out to you?

WEEKLY STUDY (30 MINS)
How is a marriage contract different than a marriage covenant?

Marriage is the hardest thing I've ever done. Being married to my bride since 1992 is the greatest thing I've ever done. Now I understand that loving her is the greatest accomplishment of my life.

How is the secular (those not living for Jesus) view of marriage different from those who are devoted to Jesus?

NOTES:

IN MEN, WE TRUST SERIES
TEAM MEETING 41 (CONT'D)

What is God's heart for marriage? How does He see it? How does he feel about divorce?
Malachi 2:13-16.

"In business and the world, we like to use contracts with the primary purpose to protect our stuff from you. It closes me OFF from you and protects me like a firewall from any litigation you may take against me. Legally the marriage is a contract but in Scripture, it is much more. It is a covenant, an opening of oneself to another with complete vulnerability and no holds barred attitude. It is all or nothing, the rubber meets the road, and the buck stops here. It is all the difference in the world. Where a contract protects my stuff from you a covenant says, "Everything I have is yours!" Marriage is such a covenant and thus a great risk. The marriage covenant is—and must always be—the line of demarcation between marriage and the marketplace."
~Wedding Ceremony Notes

Where has your marriage become little more than a contract and how do you begin fixing it?

Is there any treachery in your marriage?
Malachi 2:14

NOTES:

IN MEN, WE TRUST SERIES
TEAM MEETING 41 (CONT'D)

"How can a woman be expected to be happy with a man who insists on treating her as if she were a perfectly normal human being?"
~Oscar Wilde

In what ways can you renew your marriage with the Holy Spirit?
Malachi 2:15

"Marriages today (in and outside of the church) have a 50% chance of survival. But when couples pray regularly together that changes to about a 1 in 10,000 chance of divorce." ~Paul Friesen, *Lovin' Your Wife Like Christ When You Ain't No Jesus*

"I have learned that only two things are necessary to keep one's wife happy. First, let her think she's having her way. And second, let her have it."
~Lyndon B. Johnson

Did you know that God created marriage to last a lifetime? He hates divorce. Why?
Malachi 2:16

How do Matthew 19:3-9 and Genesis 2:18-25 support this?

"Since they are no longer two but one, let no one split apart what God has joined together." ~Matthew 19:6 (NLT)

Share a consistent, practical way you show your wife you are deeply committed to her.
1 Corinthians 7:10-14.

"All men make mistakes, but married men find out about them sooner."
~Red Skelton, Comedian

IN MEN, WE TRUST SERIES
TEAM MEETING 41 (CONT'D)

*"Let the wife make the husband glad to come home,
and let him make her sorry to see him leave."*
~Martin Luther

How can you keep the covenant with your wife daily?

What are some guardrails in the covenant relationship with one another? What practical ways (rules you live by) do you protect her?

*"There is nothing nobler or more admirable than when two people who see
eye to eye keep the house as man and wife, confounding their
enemies and delighting their friends."*
~Homer

HUDDLE TIME (10 MINS)
No Huddles Today: Instead get alone for fifteen minutes and write out how you will make your marriage a priority. Make it concrete more than philosophical. What will you do to show your wife you are hers? Keep it short and sweet. Now, do it!

NOTES:

"Marriage has no guarantees. If that's what you're looking for, go live with a car battery."
~Erma Bombeck

IN MEN, WE TRUST SERIES

TEAM MEETING 42
"SELFLESSNESS"

OPENING PRAYER (5 MINS)

HERO STORIES (5 MINS)

ROUND TABLE QUESTION (10 MINS)
In what area are you the most selfless?

WEEKLY STUDY (30 MINS)
How do you apply the following verse to selflessness?
Luke 22:24-27, John 12:24-25, and Galatians 5:13

"Every man must decide whether he will walk in the light of creative altruism or the darkness of destructive selfishness."
~Martin Luther King Jr.

NOTES:

"But to mean it when I say that I want my life to count for His glory is to drive a stake through the heart of self - a painful and determined dying to me that must be a part of every day I live."
~Louie Giglio

IN MEN, WE TRUST SERIES
TEAM MEETING 42 (CONT'D)

"But to mean it when I say that I want my life to count for His glory is to drive a stake through the heart of self - a painful and determined dying to me that must be a part of every day I live." ~Louie Giglio

Review some suggestions in our battle for selflessness from an earlier meeting.
Philippians 2:3-5

"Almost every sinful action ever committed can be traced back to a selfish motive. It is a trait we hate in other people but justify in ourselves."
~Stephen Kendrick, *The Love Dare*

What's the most difficult thing about dying to your wants and pleasures?
Romans 12:1-2, Galatians 2:20, and Galatians 6:14

Where do you need to die to your desires? Where can you be more selfless?

"Above all the grace and the gifts that Christ gives to his beloved is that of overcoming self." ~St. Francis of Assisi

HUDDLE TIME (10 MINS)
Question of the week: Share one thing you need to crucify.
"And One" Question
Pray for Each Other

NOTES:

"The mark of the immature man is that he wants to die nobly for a cause, while the mark of the mature man is that wants to live humbly for one." ~Wilhelm Stekel

TIP OF THE SPEAR SERIES

TEAM MEETING 43
"THE FORCE"

OPENING PRAYER (5 MINS)

HERO STORIES (5 MINS)

ROUND TABLE QUESTION (10 MINS)
Why are followers so important to the leader?

WEEKLY STUDY (30 MINS)
"The tip of the spear is precise, effective, efficient, guided by a force, and prepared for a specific purpose." ~Deik Maxwell

When it comes to leading spiritually, where can you demonstrate your relationship with Jesus to your family?

"The true test of a leader is whether his followers will adhere to his cause of their own volition, enduring the most arduous hardships without being forced to do so, and remaining steadfast in the moments of greatest peril."
~Xenophon, Greek historian and philosopher

NOTES:

"The tip of the spear is precise, effective, efficient, guided by a force, and prepared for a specific purpose." ~Deik Maxwell

TIP OF THE SPEAR SERIES
TEAM MEETING 43 (CONT'D)

How do we encourage those we love towards giving their lives to the great vision of following Jesus?

"The tip of the spear must head in exactly the right direction and have the entire weight of the rest behind the point. It is only the mass of what follows the point that gives the point the force to reach the desired target and penetrate it rapidly. If the point is off target, the whole thrust of the spear lies useless and idle." ~Carl Swartz

How can you speak more to your family about what God is doing in your life?

"If the mother is the first to become a Christian in a household, there is a 17% probability that everyone in the household will follow. If the father is the first to become a Christian in a household, there is a 93% probability that everyone in the household will follow." ~Baptist Press Survey, 1997

NOTES:

TIP OF THE SPEAR SERIES
TEAM MEETING 43 (CONT'D)

"The signs of outstanding leadership appear primarily among the followers. Are the followers reaching their potential? Are they learning? Serving? Do they achieve the required results? Do they change with grace? Manage conflict?"
~Max De Pree

Never shrink back from your God-given mandate to lead.
Hebrews 10:39

Why is hearing from God (and sharing it with them) so important to leading those we love?
Genesis 35:1-3

"All men dream, but not equally. Those who dream by night in the dusty recesses of their minds wake in the day to find all was vanity; but the dreamers of the day are dangerous men, for they may act on their dream with open eyes, and make it possible."
~T.E. Lawrence

What nuggets of truth can you gain about spiritual leadership?
John 4:46-53 (See verse 50)

Why is taking Jesus at his word so difficult at times?

NOTES:

TIP OF THE SPEAR SERIES
TEAM MEETING 43 (CONT'D)

What is striking about the stories of men and their households?
Acts 16:25-34 and 18:5-8

How are men the catalysts for spiritual leadership in the Bible and life?

HUDDLE TIME (10 MINS)
Question of the week: Where can you be a stronger force for God with those you love?
"And One" Question
Pray for Each Other

NOTES:

"If you think you're leading but no one is following, you're only taking a walk."
~Unknown

TIP OF THE SPEAR SERIES

TEAM MEETING 44
"THE FUNCTION"

OPENING PRAYER (5 MINS)

HERO STORIES (5 MINS)

ROUND TABLE QUESTION (10 MINS)
Share one thing you do to engage those you lead to accept and follow your core values as their own.

WEEKLY STUDY (30 MINS)
What are some things we can learn about shepherding?
John 10:1-10, Matthew 18:12-14, and Luke 15:3-7

"The Good Shepherd discourse in some respects resembles the Synoptics; both cite a parable of a shepherd and his sheep; and all three emphasize the aspect of careful concern that the shepherd feels for them. The Johannine presentation, however, is not concentrated on one point but utilizes the allegory with a wider meaning than the Synoptics. The teaching is based on the practice of sheep herding, and several aspects are utilized to create a picture of the relation of Christ to his people." ~Merrill C. Tenney Expositors Bible Commentary

What does it take for those we lead to "listen to (our) voice?" John 10:3

NOTES:

"If you don't know where you're going, you'll probably end up somewhere else." ~David Campbell

TIP OF THE SPEAR SERIES
TEAM MEETING 44 (CONT'D)

Jesus compares the shepherd to the stranger. What can we learn from this when shepherding our children or grandchildren? John 10: 4-5

A man, like a good shepherd, "lays down his life" for those under his care.
John 10:11, 17-18, 13:37-38, 15:13 and 1 John 3:16

How does sacrifice play a role in spiritual leadership?
Luke 15:3-7

"His (the shepherd's) life was very hard. No flock ever grazed without a shepherd, and he was never off duty. The shepherd's task was not only constant but dangerous, for in addition, he had to guard the flock against wild animals."
~ William Barclay Commentary

What can you gather about the Good Shepherd from the following passages?
Psalm 23:1, 77:20, 79:13, 80:1, 95:7, 100:3, Isaiah 40:11, Jeremiah 23:1, and Ezekiel 34:2

"A good leader remains focused. Controlling your destination is better than being controlled by it."
~Jack Welch

NOTES:

TIP OF THE SPEAR SERIES
TEAM MEETING 44 (CONT'D)

How can we be the gate for those we are commissioned to lead?
John 10:7-10, 14:6-7, and 1 Timothy 2:5

"There were two kinds of sheepfolds or pens. One kind was a public sheepfold found in the cities and villages. It would be large enough to hold several flocks of sheep. This sheep pen would be in the care of a porter or doorkeeper, whose duty it was to guard the door to the sheep pen during the night and to admit the shepherds in the morning. The shepherds would call their sheep, each of whom knew his own shepherd's voice, and would lead them out to pasture. The second kind of sheep pen was in the countryside, where the shepherds would keep their flocks in good weather. This type of sheep pen was nothing more than a rough circle of rocks piled into a wall with a small open space, a gate, or a door. Through it, the shepherd would drive the sheep at nightfall. Since there was no gate to close—just an opening—the shepherd would keep the sheep in and wild animals out by lying across the opening. He would sleep there, in this case becoming the door to the sheep."
~S. Michael Houdmann

What "wolves" seeking to scatter your family, must be guarded against?
John 10:11-13, Matthew 7:15-16, 10:16-17 and Acts 20:28-30

NOTES:

TIP OF THE SPEAR SERIES
TEAM MEETING 44 (CONT'D)

"A leader sees more than others see, farther than others see, and before others see."
~Leroy Eims

How is modern technology a wolf that must be defended against and how are you being proactive in regulating it? What other wolves seek to invade your home?

There are two kinds of shepherds: good shepherds and bad shepherds. What's the difference between the two?
John 10:14-18

HUDDLE TIME (10 MINS)
Question of the week: Who under your leadership care do you need to "know" more deeply?
"And One" Question
Pray for Each Other

NOTES:

"Where a man belongs is up early and alone with God seeking vision and direction for his family". ~John Piper

TIP OF THE SPEAR SERIES

TEAM MEETING 45
"THE FORGE"

OPENING PRAYER (5 MINS)

HERO STORIES (5 MINS)

ROUND TABLE QUESTION (10 MINS)
Share about a time God forged you in the furnace of suffering.

WEEKLY STUDY (30 MINS)
Before steel is forged it must be refined. How does God refine us in Scripture? Psalm 66:10, Isaiah 48:10, and Daniel 12:10

God turns our messes into His message.

No matter how dark life may seem there is always hope. God can turn our greatest tragedies into His greatest trophies.
Romans 8:18, 26-28, and 37-39

NOTES:

"If you don't know where you're going, you'll probably end up somewhere else."
~David Campbell

TIP OF THE SPEAR SERIES
TEAM MEETING 45 (CONT'D)

Pair up. Search out times in the gospels when you see Jesus forging his men through suffering.

Share your results.

> *"Leadership is forged in the furnace... He (Billy Graham) never flinched from the furnace—but let its intense heat extrude him into an extraordinary leader."*
> ~Harold Myra and Marshall Shelley, *The Leadership Secrets of Billy Graham*

In ancient times a warrior did not go down to Sporting goods stores and buy broad heads. He would start with some type of rock or volcanic glass that could be knapped into a sharp point with an antler tip. The tip of an arrow or spear would be cultivated over hours if not days to get the correct point, sharpness, and shape. The time spent cultivating this weapon assured the warrior that at the given time he would be able to utilize the fruits of his labor to either protect his family/tribe or to provide nourishment to those he loved. If the warrior neglected to shape the spearhead he would be left with just a rock. But by knapping away all of the excess rock he would be able to focus all his power into a single point.

NOTES:

> *"Nothing splendid was ever created in cold blood. Heat is required to forge anything. Every great accomplishment is the story of a flaming heart."*
> ~Arnold H. Glasow

TIP OF THE SPEAR SERIES
TEAM MEETING 45 (CONT'D)

"You cannot dream yourself into a character: you must hammer and forge yourself into one."
~Henry David Thoreau

"The origin of forging may be traced to the ancient process of hammering gold between a rock (the anvil), and a stone (the hammer). In hammering, the inertia of the fast-moving hammer provides the required deformation energy and force, while in pressing the force is static. Usually, the final shape is imparted on the workpiece by manipulating the workpiece between the flat anvil and the flat hammer as the hammer hits the workpiece repeatedly. A conical protrusion from the anvil, holes in the anvil, a variety of pegs with different cross sections, and auxiliary tools, including a large selection of shaped hand hammers, may assist the blacksmiths and their helpers."
metalforming-inc.com

NOTES:

TIP OF THE SPEAR SERIES
TEAM MEETING 45 (CONT'D)

How does God use pain and suffering to hammer us into the men He requires?
1 Peter 1:6-8, Romans 5:2-4, 8:16-18, Philippians 3:9-11, Colossians 1:24 and 2 Timothy 2:2-4

How is forging similar to pruning?
John 15:1-2

How are they different? What do you think about the promise of God found in 2 Timothy 3:10-13?

HUDDLE TIME (10 MINS)
Question of the week: Share a godly characteristic you'd like God to forge in you.
"And One" Question
Pray for Each Other

NOTES:

"Men are forged in the fires of the furnace not the comforts of the couch."
~Anonymous

TIP OF THE SPEAR SERIES

TEAM MEETING 46
"THE FALL GUY"

OPENING PRAYER (5 MINS)

HERO STORIES (5 MINS)

ROUND TABLE QUESTION (10 MINS)
What do you think of when you consider that the tip of the spear, metaphorically, is also the fall guy?

WEEKLY STUDY (30 MINS)
"The tip of the spear absorbs the impact. A man takes the hits for those he leads. Ancient arrowheads are often found broken from the impact." ~ Anonymous

Today we want to take a look at a prophecy written about Jesus over 700 years before he was born. Isaiah 53

Depending on which commentary was researched, the book of Isaiah was written sometime between 778 and 680 BCE (Before Common Era).

NOTES:

"They never fail who die for a great cause." ~George Gordon Byron

TIP OF THE SPEAR SERIES
TEAM MEETING 46 (CONT'D)

What descriptions of Jesus do you see here? Isaiah 53:1-4

Explain the word "but." Why is it there? Isaiah 53:5

What new information do we learn from Isaiah 53:5-9?
1 Peter 2:22-25, 3:18, 1 John 2:2, and 4:10

"Human progress is neither automatic nor inevitable... Every step toward the goal of justice requires sacrifice, suffering, and struggle; the tireless exertions and passionate concern of dedicated individuals." ~Martin Luther King, Jr.

"You (men) are called to sacrifice. There just isn't a way to say it any more clearly. Genuine manhood, manly manhood, and true manhood-is sacrifice."
~Steven Mansfield, *Mansfield's Book of Manly Men*

Is there something we can learn about true sacrifice?
Matthew 6:1-6, 16-18, and Luke 17:10

"One life is all we have and we live it as we believe in living it. But to sacrifice what you are and to live without belief, is a fate more terrible than dying." ~Joan of Arc

What have we learned about the sacrifice of Jesus?
Isaiah 53:10-12, Romans 3:23-24, 5:8-10, 8:17 and Titus 3:4-7

"Peace demands the most heroic labor and the most difficult sacrifice. It demands greater heroism than war. It demands greater fidelity to the truth and a much more perfect purity of conscience." ~Thomas Merton

What is the problem with being a "living sacrifice?" How do we continue to live the sacrificial life?
Romans 12:1, 1 Peter 2:5, Galatians 2:20, and 6:14

HUDDLE TIME (10 MINS)
Question of the week: How does a man keep his daily priorities in line with his deeper values?

"And One" Question

Pray for Each Other

The problem with a living sacrifice is it keeps trying to crawl off the altar!
~Unknown

WISDOM HUNTERS SERIES

TEAM MEETING 47
"PRIORITIES"

OPENING PRAYER (5 MINS)

HERO STORIES (5 MINS)

ROUND TABLE QUESTION (10 MINS)
How can a man keep the relationships he values most in the correct alignment?

WEEKLY STUDY (30 MINS)

"The foundation of every family is the husband and wife. If they don't make that foundation their priority, then everything else will receive too much, or too little attention. The children are not the center of the family. You and your spouse are the centers, and if the center of your marriage doesn't hold, everything else in your family is going to fall apart."
~Dr. Kevin Leman, Bring Home the Joy

Hand your Huddle Partner your smartphone. What three things seem to dominate your calendar as core values?

NOTES:

"When I ask the wife almost invariably I hear that the number one priority in her husband's life is his job." ~Dr. Kevin Leman, Bring Home the Joy

WISDOM HUNTERS SERIES
TEAM MEETING 47 (CONT'D)

How can you make it unmistakably clear that you value family (marriage first) over your career?

"I've never heard a dying man say, 'I wish I'd spent more time at the office."
~Lee Iacocca

"Communicate with your wife. Listen to her heart more than words. You don't always have to be right." ~Bill Osborne, The Original 15, Men in the Arena

How does the following verse speak about the prioritized life and our family legacy? Matthew 13:7-9 and 22-23 and John 12:23-24

How can we relate the following passages to the relationship with our wife and children? Matthew 6:19-21 and 16:24-27

What does it take for a man to leave a Christian legacy behind?
Exodus 20:5-6, 34:7 and Numbers 14:18

HUDDLE TIME (10 MINS)
Question of the week: How would your wife/children disagree with how you prioritize your life? Why?
"And One" Question
Pray for Each Other

NOTES:

"Perception is reality when those we're charged to love and lead spiritually see themselves as second to our career." ~Anonymous

WISDOM HUNTERS SERIES
TEAM MEETING 48
"RISKY BUSINESS"

OPENING PRAYER (5 MINS)

HERO STORIES (5 MINS)

ROUND TABLE QUESTION (10 MINS)
Share your thoughts on this statement: "The older we become, the more difficult it is to risk it all for God."

WEEKLY STUDY (30 MINS)

*"Accept the fact that failure is not only an option,
it's a reality when we are willing to risk it all for the Master."*
~Anonymous

If someone gave you a million dollars with the only stipulation that the money had to be used for any Kingdom cause, what would you do with it? Dream big.

In his book *The Kingdom of God is a Party*, Dr. Tony Campolo surveyed fifty 95-year-olds asking what they would change if they could go back and live life over again. Risking more in life was one of the top three answers.

NOTES:

"If you want to walk on water, you have to be willing to get your feet wet first. Then you discover it is worth the risk." ~John Ortberg

WISDOM HUNTERS SERIES
TEAM MEETING 48 (CONT'D)

Read the story of Peter walking on water. Overlooking his obvious flaws, what is it about Peter that resonates with men?
Matthew 14:22-33.

In spending time with patients during the last weeks of their lives, Australian palliative care nurse Bronnie Ware gleaned vital insight into the concerns and regrets of those faced with imminent death. In *The Five Most Common Regrets of Living and Dying*, she found that two of the five most common regrets of all were, "The courage to live true to myself, not the life others expected of me" and "The courage to express my feelings." Both of these involve taking great risks.

What encouragement to take great risks do you find in Peter?
Matthew 14:22-33, Joshua 1:5-9, Matthew 28:20, and Hebrews 13:5

The rubber meets the road, or should we say the sandals meet the sea. What went wrong?
Matthew 14:28-31.

"If things seem under control, you are just not going fast enough."
~Mario Andretti, Race Car Driver

NOTES:

"Only those who will risk going too far can find out how far one can go."
~T. S. Eliot

WISDOM HUNTERS SERIES
TEAM MEETING 48 (CONT'D)

What went right for Peter on the water?

What kind of storms prevent men from risking it all to walk on the water?

"Twenty years from now you will be more disappointed by the things that you didn't do than by the ones you did do, so throw off the bowlines, sail away from safe harbor, and catch the trade winds in your sails. Explore. Dream. Discover."
~Mark Twain

How does the fear of failure keep men in the boat?

"I've missed more than 9000 shots in my career. I've lost almost 300 games. Twenty-six times I've been trusted to take the game-winning shot and missed. I've failed over and over and over again in my life. And that is why I succeed."
~Michael Jordan, Clothing Commercial

"The best time to plant a tree was twenty years ago. The second best time is now."
~Chinese Proverb

How long do the storms usually last? What lesson can we learn from this?
Matthew 14:32-33

"There is only one way to avoid criticism: do nothing, say nothing, and be nothing." ~Aristotle

NOTES:

"Don't worry about failures, worry about the chances you miss when you don't even try."
~Jack Canfield

WISDOM HUNTERS SERIES
TEAM MEETING 48 (CONT'D)

What's the worst that can happen if your dream doesn't work out the way you hoped? Which one resonates the most?

"Don't be too timid and squeamish about your actions. All life is an experiment. The more experiments you make the better."
~Ralph Waldo Emerson

What other fears are preventing you for taking the risk you've been talking about? What is the worst that can happen?

"Do one thing every day that scares you."
~Eleanor Roosevelt

What if God really does answer your prayers?

"Pearls don't lie on the seashore. If you want one, you must dive for it."
~Chinese Proverb

HUDDLE TIME (10 MINS)
Question of the week: What are you waiting for?
"And One" Question
Pray for Each Other

NOTES:

"Go out on a limb. That's where the fruit is." ~Jimmy Carter

WISDOM HUNTERS SERIES

TEAM MEETING 49
"LEGACY LIVING"

OPENING PRAYER (5 MINS)

HERO STORIES (5 MINS)

ROUND TABLE QUESTION (10 MINS)
When you die, how will your loved ones eulogize you?

WEEKLY STUDY (30 MINS)
When he was 13, Peter Drucker's teacher asked his class what they wanted to be remembered for, but none could answer. The teacher said, "I didn't expect you to be able to respond, but if you still can't by the time your 50, you've wasted your life." This one question changed his life.

The goal today is for you to see the end of your life. Discuss the quote by Matthew Henry.

NOTES:

"It ought to be the business every day to prepare for the final day." ~Matthew Henry

WISDOM HUNTERS SERIES
TEAM MEETING 49 (CONT'D)

A Man of Legacy.

"Jonathan Edwards was one man who made a difference. Born in 1703, he was perhaps the most brilliant mind America had ever produced. A pastor, a writer, and later, the president of Princeton, he and his wife had eleven children. Of his known male descendants: more than 300 became pastors, missionaries, or theological professors, 120 were professors at various universities, 110 became attorneys, sixty were prominent authors, thirty were judges, fourteen served as presidents of universities and colleges, three served in the U.S. Congress; and one became vice-president of the United States."
~Steve Farrar, *Point Man*

On your deathbed, what regrets do you want to avoid?

In his book *The Kingdom of God is a Party*, Dr. Tony Campolo surveyed fifty 95-year-olds asking what they would change if they could go back and live life over again. Doing things that would live on after death, legacy, was one of the top three answers.

What do the following passages teach us about legacy?
Exodus 20:5-6, 34:7 and Numbers 14:18

NOTES:

WISDOM HUNTERS SERIES
TEAM MEETING 49 (CONT'D)

"Have you ever noticed how many men in the bible failed in the second half of life? Our enemy is so cunning that he will wait forty or even fifty years to set a trap."
~Joe Aldrich

We know from Scripture that Satan desires to steal, kill, and destroy us (John 10:10a). How are these three different?
Galatians 5:15, Hebrews 10:38-39 and 1 Peter 5:8

"He wants to destroy you. He wants your lineage, your spiritual family tree, to die with you. If he can kill the faith of your children, then he's succeeded in destroying your eternal legacy. Does this need an explanation? Finishing strong means more than just finishing. It means taking others with us to heaven."
~Jim Ramos, *The Field Guide: A Bathroom Book for Men*

What legacy events/traditions can you create in your family?

Have you done any rites of passage into adulthood with your sons or daughters? Why?

Take the rest of today's Team Meeting and write the obituary you'd like to have written about you.

"An obituary is a news article that reports the recent death of a person, typically along with an account of the person's life and information about the upcoming funeral. In large cities and larger newspapers, obituaries are written only for people considered significant. In local newspapers, an obituary may be published for any resident upon death." ~Wikipedia

HUDDLE TIME (10 MINS)
Question of the week: If you died today, what legacy of faith would you have left with those you love?
"And One" Question. Pray for Each Other.

WISDOM HUNTERS SERIES
TEAM MEETING 49 (CONT'D)

MY OBITUARY:

"If the young are not initiated into the village, they will burn it down just to feel its warmth."
~African Proverb

WISDOM HUNTERS SERIES

TEAM MEETING 50
"SEE THE FINISH"

OPENING PRAYER (5 MINS)

HERO STORIES (5 MINS)

ROUND TABLE QUESTION (10 MINS)
Ending something is different than finishing strong because...

WEEKLY STUDY (30 MINS)
Here we are! Our last meeting of the Men's Ministry Playbook. During our journey together, you have probably witnessed close to 20% of the men who verbally committed (gave their word) quit, throw in the towel, give up, and become victims of attrition. But you were not one of them. Congratulations. You have just qualified yourself for the next step—launching a team of your own!

What separates men from finishing strong from those who finish wrong? Think about times you quit too quickly. Is there a deciding factor?

"Protecting integrity, fighting apathy, pursuing God passionately, leading courageously, and finishing strong?" ~Jim Ramos, Definition of Manhood, *Strong Men Dangerous Times*

NOTES:

"We shall neither fail nor falter; we shall not weaken or tire... give us the tools and we will finish the job." ~Winston Churchill

WISDOM HUNTERS SERIES
TEAM MEETING 50 (CONT'D)

The name Mickey Thompson used to be one of the most recognized names in auto racing. His team could build the fastest cars on the track. They could fly! It's interesting, though, that not one of those cars ever brought Thompson the checkered flag. His cars took the lead in the first 29 races they entered, but they never won a race. They never finished! Thompson could build the fastest cars, but not cars that would last. Engines blew. Gearboxes broke. Carburetors failed. The cars began as good starters and quick runners but were not good for the distance.

Silently read Numbers 13:1-24.

> *"Successful men keep moving. They make mistakes, but they don't quit."*
> ~Conrad Hilton

Now, take turns reading the spies' report, specifically Caleb's response. What insight can you gain about Caleb the man?
Numbers 13:25-33

The people rebel against God and Caleb responds by tearing his clothes. Why?
Numbers 14:1-10

NOTES:

> *"Don't quit till the job is done—finish."*
> ~Stu Weber

WISDOM HUNTERS SERIES
TEAM MEETING 50 (CONT'D)

"Primarily associated with mourning, such tearing of the clothes was an expression of deep sorrow and heartfelt grief. It was also a natural reaction at times of great distress and in cases of sincere repentance."
~Bible Gateway

Because of their disobedience, God prohibited the Hebrews from entering the Promised Land, except Joshua and Caleb. What "spirit" did they possess that set them apart in God's eyes?
Numbers 14:24, 38, 26:64-65 and 32:11-12

"A man can travel 7,000 miles around the world, but it's the last thirty inches that matter."
~Don Owens

How does having this spirit help a man to finish strong?
2 Timothy 4:6-7

What insights can you gain about what qualities Caleb possessed that helped him finish so well?
Joshua 14:6-14

NOTES:

"True courage is taking another small step each day toward achieving your vision."
~Jonathan Lockwood Huie

WISDOM HUNTERS SERIES
TEAM MEETING 50 (CONT'D)

"Our churches have fallen into the unfortunate situation of losing far too many of our seniors who have a significant amount of time and experience to offer to younger generations. This is happening because we have fallen prey to someone wrongfully telling seniors to pass the baton. Please do not tell me to pass the baton unless the message you want to relay is that I no longer have any value.
If you have bought into the lie and passed the baton, take it back!
God will tell you when you are done."
~Chuck Stecker

"Habit is a cable; we weave a thread of it each day, and at last, we cannot break it."
~Horace Mann

What truth is there in the belief that our life will only be as strong as how strong we finish each day?

"Do not plan for ventures before finishing what's at hand."
~Euripides

HUDDLE TIME (10 MINS)
Question of the week: What one habit have you formed that's helping you finish life strong? What's one that's hurting you?
"And One" Question
Pray for Each Other

NOTES:

"It's hard to beat a person who never gives up." ~Babe Ruth

THE MEN'S MINISTRY PLAYBOOK

DIVIDE AND CONQUER: DO IT AGAIN

Our hope these fifty weeks together have been transformative for you and those you love. Remember, we believe that when a man gets it—everyone wins! Please reach out to us and let us know how God has used our humble material to impact you deeply. We find great joy in celebrating lives changed through the power of God.

Through the pages of this book, we have been forthright about our desired next steps for all men using our materials. You have most likely been paired with another man and sat under the leadership of two other men and committed "learners."

The next step of your three-phase journey is to become a leader (co-leader actually) with a team of your own. Simply connect with our team to get support. You need and follow the steps outlined in this book. You've already gone through the material. Starting your group is a no-brainer. You've got this! We believe in you. We know that you have what it takes to have an exceptional team. You are supposed to be here, reading this.

Now is the time to act!

THE MEN'S MINISTRY PLAYBOOK
ACKNOWLEDGMENTS

You may have noticed I use the words **our, we,** and **us** throughout this book. It is strategic. We decided this would be a self-published resource for various reasons and used our great team to get this resource into your hands. It is not about the man, it is about the mission, and many have teamed up on this project to drive the mission of Men in the Arena onward and upward.

Shanna without you there would be no Men in the Arena. You are the strongest, bravest, and most faithful person I know. Don't get me started on your beauty. You already know how I feel. I love you more and more throughout the years. You have made me better. I love you.

My Board of Directors continues to lead the way in ministry, wisdom, and resources. Leadership can be a lonely place but thanks to you, men, it has been a joy. Thank you to **Mike Goins, Gary McCusker, Pat George, Jeff Dyck, John Kent,** and **Fred Workman. Ken Watson** has gone through every team meeting multiple times as a team leader and editor since 2013. Ken, your advice, critiques, and advice have been instrumental. You are a man I hope to emulate in the coming years, and you have a few on me yet!

Jay Penton is a retired Alabama State Trooper and the newest member of our ministry team who is responsible for Global outreach and church relationships. His job is simple. Start new teams. He has scrutinized this book to make sure it will be a high-value asset to churches, first responders, active military, and men in underdeveloped nations. Thanks for your heart, brother.

Sam Gipson is the husband of our Digital Marketing and Collaboration Director who is passionate about men's ministry. He not only runs a large group of men in his local church but plays a massive role on key social media platforms. He has not been asked to get eyes on this project but I am thinking of him nonetheless. I know he will rip the manuscript out of his bride's hands. Thank you for your brilliant mind, man!

Lastly, I want to thank the person who put this book together, **Caitlin Gipson**. From the days when you were in my youth group until now, you continue to be a servant, hard charger, and devoted follower of Jesus. You have put our ministry on the map because of your exceptional drive and creativity. Though you are 1,000 miles away you continue to challenge, push, and make things better. Now the world knows that Men in the Arena's right-hand man...is a woman!

THE MEN'S MINISTRY PLAYBOOK

ABOUT JIM RAMOS

Jim Ramos is a bestselling author, speaker, and the founder of Men in the Arena, a non-profit Christian ministry focused on equipping men to honor God in the leadership of their family, church, and community.

He hosts the #1 ranked Spotify podcast for Christian men, the Men in the Arena Podcast, interviewing experts in Christian manhood and partnering with thought-leaders like John Eldredge, Gary Chapman, Gene Getz, Patrick Morley, and Emerson Eggerichs.

Called "one of the pioneers of digital men's ministry," Ramos leads an army of 300,000 men on social media, founded the 17,000-strong Men in the Arena Facebook Group, and established a global network of Men in the Arena virtual teams, where men support each other as they work to become their best version.

He has written numerous books, including the #1 Amazon Bestseller *Strong Men Dangerous Times*; *The Field Guide: A Bathroom Book for Men*; *Tell Them: What Great Fathers Tell Their Sons and Daughters*; the five-book *Strong Men Study Guide Series* for small groups, and releasing September of 2024 with David C Cook Publishing, *Dialed In: Reaching Your Full Capacity as a Man of God*.

Jim lives in McMinnville, Oregon, with his wife Shanna. His goal is to live each day to its fullest with courageous abandon according to Jesus' promise in John 10:10. He loves to hunt with his adult sons, enjoy the fitness lifestyle, take tropical vacations with Shanna, and listen to men share their stories over a dark roasted Americano.

Connect with Jim on Instagram or TikTok @themeninthearena. Submit your Hero Story describing how your life has changed by going through this study at info@meninthearena.org.

meninthearena.org